Blender for
Visual Effects

Blender for
Visual Effects

Sam Vila

CRC Press
Taylor & Francis Group
Boca Raton London New York

CRC Press is an imprint of the
Taylor & Francis Group, an **informa** business

AN A K PETERS BOOK

CRC Press
Taylor & Francis Group
6000 Broken Sound Parkway NW, Suite 300
Boca Raton, FL 33487-2742

© 2015 by Taylor & Francis Group, LLC
CRC Press is an imprint of Taylor & Francis Group, an Informa business

No claim to original U.S. Government works

Printed on acid-free paper
Version Date: 20150421

International Standard Book Number-13: 978-1-4987-2450-0 (Pack - Book and Ebook)

Library of Congress Cataloging-in-Publication Data

Vila, Sam.
    Blender for visual effects / Sam Vila.
        pages cm
    Includes index.
    Summary: "This book explains how to use Blender to create visual effects, for animated film and game development, i.e., how to set up cameras on a stage, lighting and other production processes using Blender. While there are many Blender books on the market, they are more generic and cover animation, rendering, and compositing. This book takes a focused look at how to create visual effects (VFX) using Blender. The author uses many practical examples throughout to illustrate how to use Blender tools and features for scene tracking, setup, rendering, masking, and other post-production functions in a visual effects environment"-- Provided by publisher.
        ISBN 978-1-4987-2450-0
    1. Blender (Computer file) 2. Computer animation. 3. Computer graphics. 4. Three-dimensional display systems. I. Title.

TR897.72.B55V53 2015
006.6'96--dc23   2014047995

Visit the Taylor & Francis Web site at
http://www.taylorandfrancis.com

and the CRC Press Web site at
http://www.crcpress.com

Contents

Acknowledgments

I have the opportunity to write a personal message, so I would like to thank some people.

Especially I want to thank my mother and the rest of my family for always being on my side and giving me support. They taught me valuable lessons that will remain part of me for the rest of my life.

I want to thank as well my closest friends for their support throughout my career.

Thanks to Jesse Moons for helping me with this book. He allowed me to use his acting skills to create the example for this book.

I want to mention as well the Blender Community for making this such a special experience. Blender is not only a software but a different way of thinking in many ways. Our community is very special, in particular Los Angeles Blender Group for all their support. Thanks, JT Nelson, not only for your help with my book but also for your great effort in making our community bigger and stronger.

Finally I want to thank you for choosing this book. Blender is getting better and better every day and new opportunities are becoming available to Blender users. More and more interesting projects of all kinds are choosing Blender in their pipeline, and that is one of the reasons I decided to write this book—to help people get involved with Blender in a professional way and to promote this fantastic program.

Thanks.

Sam Vila

Biography

Sam Vila earned a filmmaking certificate from the London Film Academy in 2006 and other degrees from different schools for film editing, camera operation, Steadicam operation, and postproduction.

He has been progressing in his career as a filmmaker and visual effects artist by participating in several productions not only for television but also for feature films.

Currently Sam Vila is working as a visual effects artist in Los Angeles, California, using Blender as the main tool to generate all the visual effects on a daily basis.

His experience includes five feature films and several short films usually as a visual effects artist. With several years of experience creating 3D content, he has wide-ranging knowledge of many well-known 3D software programs, and he has engaged in professional collaborations with companies such as NVIDIA and OTOY (Octane Render).

He is also a cofounder of Los Angeles Blender Group and a very active member of the Blender community.

1
PROBLEM DEFINITION

In this book we are going to see the different techniques used in a visual effects production, with an example of how to use Blender to accomplish postproduction work from start to finish in a professional workflow while trying to cover the most common aspects we could find in a video/film production.

Introduction

The purpose of this book is to show how to use the most common tools used in the film and video industry such as tracking, rendering, compositing, and others. We will also discuss how to deal with limitations and sort out problems to achieve the completion of our project. To do that, we are going to follow an example project, starting with how to prepare the elements that we will need later on, how to render the plates, and how to composite all the elements together in the right way.

Composition is the most important topic in this book. In these pages we will examine all the compositing nodes we can use in Blender. In addition, we will look at some interesting tips, features such as the motion tracker, and rendering techniques so we can have enough information to accomplish the most common tasks we will encounter in the creation of a professional visual effects composition.

Approaching the Task

The best way to learn something is with a practical example, and in this book we will look at problematic scenarios in a common production with an eye to getting through all the stages of the project until we complete it.

For this task in particular I chose a scene that I shot myself, having in mind that with this example scene we can cover most of the common works and techniques in a production. We are going to cover many aspects, such as how to shoot a scene in the right way, how to track and set up the scene in Blender, and finally how to composite all the elements.

You will find as well a detailed explanation of the compositing nodes with examples for each of them during the last part of the book. This will help not only the beginners but also the advanced users of Blender by using it as a node reference guide.

Additional Materials

Additional materials are available from the CRC Press website. Look under the "Downloads/Updates" tab at http://www.crcpress.com/product/isbn/9781498724500.

Summary

The main goal of this book is to help the user understand the limitations of the software and how to sort out problems, keeping in mind the example scene to cover most of the aspects in a film/video production. But the most important thing for the user to learn is how to be sufficiently capable in a wide range of situations.

2
PREPARATION

In this chapter we are going to make sure we have all the elements we need to start working on a project.

Getting Ready

It's quite obvious that if this book is about Blender, we need the software we're talking about, so let's pick it up from the official website: http://www.blender.org.

Once you are on the main page, click on the download section and select the distribution for your operating system. Install the software once the download is finished and then you're ready to go.

Here is an example of how the main interface of Blender appears:

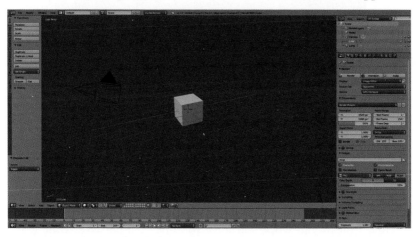

During the creative process of this book, we used Blender 2.72a so it's important that you have at least this version or newer to follow all the instructions in this book without trouble. If you use an older version, you might not have all the features needed in this book to complete the lessons.

Setting up Blender

Now that you have Blender up and running, we should spend a couple of minutes to set up a few things in Blender that will allow us to work in a much more efficient way for these kinds of projects. To do that, we need to go to **File** and then click on **User Preferences**. A new window will open so we can adjust almost anything we want in Blender.

The main thing we need to change is the memory cache limit due to the fact that we are going to work with high-resolution footage later on. By default it is set to 128 megabytes, but we should increase this value almost to the maximum supported by our operating system. In my case I have 16 gigabytes of RAM, which is 16,384 megabytes, but I'm going to set my memory cache to about 13 gigabytes (13,312 megabytes) so I leave about 3 gigabytes for the operating system and other resources.

QUICK TIP: You should make sure you have your display calibrated for any professional work you have to deliver; otherwise, your work might look completely offset in colors or gamma and other settings from one device to another. The best way to get the right settings is with a hardware calibrator. These devices are not cheap, but it's the way to go if you really want to handle professional works.

Shooting

For this book I recorded some footage with the help of an actor, and I set up the scene in a way that allows me to show you different techniques used in real productions.

The main thing I needed for my scene was a green background with some tracking marks, lit up in a way that creates green even areas. Make sure to set up your actor or element at some distance from the green screen or else the light will bounce and will turn the green screen into a green light source, causing color spill.

We can use a blue screen instead of a green screen in case our actor has to wear some green elements. Either option is fine, but green screens are recommended due to the fact that some cameras store more information in the green channel than in the blue channel, making it much easier to remove the green background.

Sometimes it is not possible to have a perfect green screen set, but we can fix some issues later on in postproduction, as we will see in later chapters.

It is also important for this example to have some areas and elements to track so we need to place some static elements that can be tracked without interfering with the main subject, in this case the actor. We can use almost anything that remains static. We should place the elements we want to track at different distances so we can provide enough information to the tracking software later on. (Our example includes "+" tape marks on the far wall and a white ball on a stand closer to the actor.) This method for placing the elements will bring us a good parallax effect so the tracker can solve the distances in a much more accurate way.

As a final note I would suggest getting as much information as you can during the shooting process, especially some measurement information like the distances between tracking elements, or the distance between the sensor of our camera and the target. Also it's really important to know what focal length has been used during the filming.

Calibration

One of the most important things to have before we jump into the software side is to have all of the elements that we want to work with in the right format. We talked about having even areas of green or blue background if you have to deal with background removal and also we mentioned the importance of parallax and collecting as many measurements as possible during the set.

For tracking, one really important piece of information to collect is the lens distortion index. All the lenses have a distortion factor due to the fact that lenses are usually built with convex and/or concave elements, which causes the light to get distorted when the sensor inside the camera collects the rays. We need to know how much distortion is caused by our lenses, and the best way is to use a calibration sheet like this:

This grid shows flat lines, and we will use this to see how much distortion is caused by the lenses in our camera. There are many calibration sheets, but I suggest that you use this 10 × 10 grid as it is the same one that Blender uses to calibrate the tracking. However, you could use similar ones.

Once you have your calibration sheet printed, all you have to do is glue it onto a flat surface that is stiff enough to prevent any distorted lines. Then, put this calibration grid in front of the camera, covering all of your frame before you shoot your scene. This way, you will know how much distortion is being created by your lens. We will see later on how to use this grid in Blender.

Summary

In this chapter we saw how to start setting up all the necessary elements that we will need in subsequent chapters. The next chapters will demonstrate a practical way to learn how to use Blender's tools in the most common scenarios, but before that we needed to make sure we had everything set up in the right way to avoid problems in the future.

3
TRACKING

In this chapter we will start working with Blender. This is a very important chapter and one of the most difficult ones to master. To learn how to track a shot perfectly might require an entire book and much time practicing. It's hard to fit all the techniques about tracking in one chapter, but we will cover the basics and some tips.

Basics of Tracking

For people who are not familiar with this term, I would define this technique as the reconstruction of a real scene into a CG scene by re-creating the movement of a physical camera and transferring the information of each movement into keyframes in a 3D world. This is a very interesting and powerful tool for these kinds of visual effects projects. It allows us to integrate real environments and elements into our project so we can do many tricks later on with them.

Previously we had to use external programs for tracking because Blender didn't have this feature, but the Blender Foundation added this functionality into their software. This opens a new world of possibilities and options into this wonderful software, as we no longer need to use any external software for these kinds of jobs, and it provides very nice and tight integration.

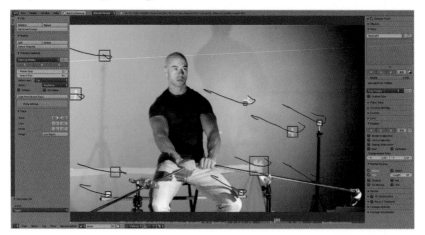

Preparing the Footage

Let's consider a couple of suggestions before we start working with the tracking system.

The most important one is to remember to have at least eight elements to track in our footage. Sometimes some of these elements get occluded or just don't track well enough so we need to make sure we will have at least eight elements to track *all the time* later on.

Another important thing is to get as much information about what we use in the real scene so we can transfer all this information into the 3D scene later on. For example, it is very important to know the type of camera we are going to use, the focal length, the sensor size, and some other measurements. For these additional measurements, it would be interesting, if possible, to measure the distances between key elements so we can tell Blender the exact distances between the tracking points. Then, we can re-create the scene in a much more accurate way.

In the previous chapter I mentioned parallax. This is one of the keys to a good tracking solution. *Parallax* is used to explain the different distances we perceive when we see objects. If we place the marks to be tracked on the same area and distance from the camera, the result is not going to be good enough for some projects so we need to provide additional information to the tracker by placing some elements at different distances to provide the depth information to the tracking solver to re-create the scene. In the example scene, we placed some stands next to the character without occluding the area we are going to use later on. However, by doing this, we provide more elements to track and we make sure we are going to have a good parallax for the tracking solver.

Finally I would suggest the use of contrasted elements. This means using elements that are easy to perceive by the tracker and trying to avoid similar colors between the elements to track and the background; otherwise, it will be very easy for the tracker to lose the tracked element.

NOTE: In the example for this book, I intentionally prepared the footage in a simple way and far from the very best conditions. This helps to show some of the common problems in some productions and to shows how to solve these problems. It is likely that sometimes you could be working with footage that contains such problematic elements.

Working with the Tracker

Time to do some tracking in Blender. First thing we need to do is set up the scene units in Blender. We can select the unit type we want to use by going to the **Scene** button and clicking on the **Metric** button. This will help us later on to get the right values when we work with 3D elements.

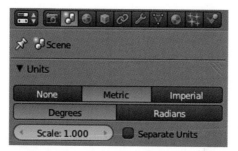

Now let's go to the tracking panel. Click on the **Editor Type** button and select **Movie Clip Editor**. The interface will change into the tracking interface.

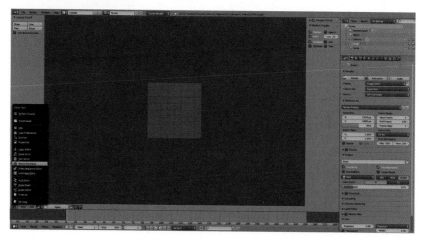

Click on the **Open** button and select the footage you are going to use. Usually Blender works better with image sequences for this kind of task and JPEG format is faster than others (e.g., PNG) but the quality is not as good, so sometimes you need to think what would be best for your project.

We can click on the **Prefetch** button to load all the frames into the memory RAM. That way, instead of reading the frames from the hard drive, which is quite slow, it will read the frames from the RAM, speeding up the playback and the tracking as well. We can also click on the **Set Scene Frames** button, and Blender will automatically set the start and end frame in our project based on the length of the footage we loaded.

We can also build a proxy (lower-quality) version of our original footage to work much faster and then switch to the original footage when we want higher quality. To do this, we can go to the right-side panel in the **Proxy** section, select the options you want to generate the proxy version, and click on the **Build Proxy** button. It will take a little while to generate the proxy, but this will allow us to work much faster in the long run.

We can swap the footage from the original to the proxy one by clicking on the **Proxy render size** button.

Now we can play the footage with the combination **Alt+A**. If you want to just use a portion of your footage, you can easily set up the start and end for your footage by pressing the S key for the starting position and the **E** key for the ending position.

Calibration inside Blender

Recall in the previous chapter when we prepared the calibration sheet. Now we are going to use the lens distortion information we collected, thanks to the calibration sheet we prepared previously.

Once we have our footage loaded and before we start tracking the marks, we should go to the **Display** section and click on **Grid**. We should then see something like this:

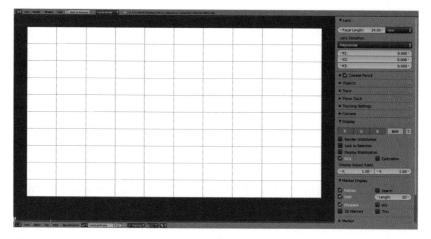

These lines should match the ones from our footage when we had the calibration sheet in front of the camera. It's quite possible that the lines on your footage are not completely straight as these ones, so to adjust these lines we have to adjust the values in the **Lens** section where it says K1, K2, and K3.

Once we have the values that make the lines in Blender match the footage, we should see the grid distorted as in this example:

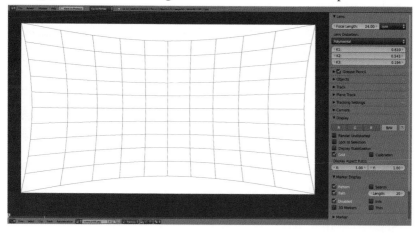

Now we can notice how much the lens we used in our footage distorted the light rays when these ones hit our sensor. The reason for doing this procedure is that the render engines usually cannot simulate the lens distortion from a real camera in our viewport and also doesn't know how much distortion to apply so we are building this information to use it later on during our pipeline.

Once we have the right distortion values, we should create an undistorted proxy or video with the previously mentioned proxy panel so we can use the undistorted footage in our 3D viewport and we can align our 3D geometry in the right way. For the moment we can disable the grid in the display section and continue with our tracking.

Placing the Marks

It's time to place the tracking marks. To do this, we just need to press the **Ctrl** (control) key and click on any area we want to track and we will notice that a new element shows up in the viewport:

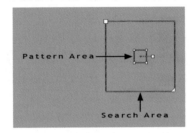

This is a tracking point and it's defined by two main areas: the pattern area and the search area. The *pattern area* is the area that the tracker is going to try to find in the previous or next frames of your footage.

Then we have the *search area*, which is used by the tracker to define an area in which to look for the pattern area in other frames. To turn on the search area in the viewport, go to the right panel in the **Marker Display** section and click on the **Search** button.

This is very important because sometimes you want to define an area to search to avoid undesired results. It also makes the calculations much faster as the tracker doesn't need to find the pattern area in the entire frame but just in the limited area we chose as the search area.

Smaller search areas are faster to calculate than bigger ones. It might not sound important, but if you need to track several elements during many frames and with some high-quality footage, you may need to keep this in mind. Continue placing trackers for the rest of the frames. You can use the timeline to choose a better place to use the trackers.

We can use the same shortcuts that are used with other elements in Blender, so we can use **G** to grab a tracking point, **S** to scale, **R** to rotate, and **A** to select all the tracking points; press **A** again to deselect. Once we finish placing all the marks we need, we can select one or more tracking marks, and in the left-side panel we can find the **Track** section:

With this panel we can start tracking the markers we have already placed on the entire footage. We can track a marker forward until it stops or backward until it stops, but also we can track frame by frame in both directions for finer control. This panel also allows us to clear portions of tracking data for the marks based on the actual frame.

A common problem with the tracking is that sometimes the reference pattern area is lost for apparently no reason, but there's actually a reason: the accuracy we try to get with that particular mark. By default the accuracy correlation is set to 0.750, but sometimes we need to drop it a little bit so we can continue using that particular tracker. To do this, we need to go to the **Tracking Settings** section on the right-side panel.

The most important parameter here is the correlation. As stated previously, it's set to 0.750 by default, but we can adjust this parameter to get more precise tracking in our marker by increasing this setting up to 1 or less precise by decreasing to 0. Don't drop this value too much as it will produce a less accurate solution. Usually a little bit lower than the default is fine.

If our tracking point is still failing, we should try to move the point a little bit or change the size of the pattern area or the search area a little bit. There's no magic setting for that, but sometimes it's necessary to tweak these settings and retrack the marker until it completes the entire range of frames we want. The **Motion model** and the **Match** options are also very critical to get the right tracking. Try **Affine** and **Previous frame**, respectively, in case you run into problems. These are usually the most precise settings.

Solving the Tracking

We should have now a good number of accurate tracking points, so we can proceed to the camera solving process. In this stage Blender is going to collect all the information about our tracking marks and is going to calculate how the distances between the tracking marks are performing in the real-life footage and will provide a simulated version of the real camera movement so we can apply it to our 3D camera.

First we need to tell Blender how to calculate the distance and the movement of these points, so we need to go to the right-side panel and fill as much information as we can on the **Camera** section:

If you are not sure about these settings, you can use the **Camera Presets** button or look for the specifications of your camera in the camera's manual or on the Internet. It's important to fill the parameters correctly so that our simulation will be more accurate.

At the other side of the viewport, we need now to go to the **Solve** section. In this section there are very interesting settings that will help us get a good result.

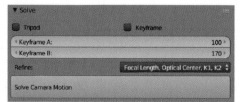

We need to define a range of frames with enough movement to provide the best information to the calculation. Here we return to the concept of parallax. That is why it was so important to define previously, because now is its critical moment. We need to look through our footage to find a range of frames with enough parallax and movement to get as much information as Blender needs to generate the 3D camera.

There's no standard value for this, so you need to find in your footage a good starting frame and end frame, and then type the values of these frames in the boxes **Keyframe A** for the starting frame and **Keyframe B** for the ending frame. We can also check the **Keyframe** option if we want Blender to calculate this for us.

Finally we click on the **Solve Camera Motion** button, and Blender will start the calculation process. It will take a little while to complete the job. We won't see many things happening after that, because it does the work internally. The most important thing to keep an eye on is this value:

Solve error reveals the accuracy of the calculations generated based on our settings. A value above 1.0 means that the solution calculated is not as accurate as it should be, so we would have some problems during the next stages; we don't want that, so try to avoid going higher than 1.0. A value lower than 1.0 should be good enough for what we need, while a value much higher than 1.0 would be totally unacceptable.

If we still have values above 1.0, then we need to tweak a few things and recalculate the camera movement in the **Solve** panel.

The most common problem is having a tracking point that is not accurate enough. To check this, we can go back to the right-side panel in the **Track** section and we should see at the bottom an **Average Error** part. It works very similarly to the previous setting.

If it is above 1.0, the tracking point is not sufficiently accurate; however, it's less critical than the overall solved camera calculation, so we could use values above 1.0 if we still have some other tracking points with good values. We could use tracking points with values up to 2.0 more or less, but we should avoid use tracking points with a value near 3.0 or higher.

We should check all our track points one by one to make sure we only use the most accurate ones in the calculation on the **Solve** panel. If you notice some tracking points with high values, you should delete or disable the problematic ones.

There is also an interesting option on the left toolbar called **Clean up**, which highlights the markers with the values we want to delete. This will help us to find the wrong markers instead of checking them manually one by one.

Another way to increase the precision of our camera solution is with the **Refine** section on the **Solve** panel:

There are different options for a particular problem in this menu. Blender autocorrects some values, but this may affect the accuracy of the original parameters we provided, so make sure the values provided by this feature are what you are looking for.

Applying the Solved Camera

Let's return to the 3D viewport. I suggest that you split the view, as we will still work a little bit more with the tracking interface and we will need the 3D viewport as well.

Now that we are on the 3D viewport, let's change to the camera view by pressing **0** on the numeric keypad. Then, in the tracking interface, click on the **Set as Background** on the **Scene Setup** section in the left panel.

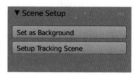

We should see now how our footage is shown through the 3D camera in Blender; however, we don't have any motion in that camera yet, so we need to apply the tracking solution to the 3D camera. To do this, we need to select the camera and go to the **Object constraints** button and then click on **Add Object Constraint** and select **Camera Solver**:

If we play back our animation now in the 3D viewport, we would notice that something is happening now with the camera, and we can even see the tracking points working as they should. However, the axis or the scale might be wrong, so we need to set up these things to make sure we are on the right track for the next stage.

Go back to the tracking interface and click on the bottom menu in the **Reconstruction** option.

In this menu we will set up the axis and the main size of the scene. Let's start with the origin of our scene. To do this, we just need to select one of our tracking marks and then click **Set Origin** in the **Reconstruction** menu. We should notice how the 3D viewport has changed.

Next we define the floor. For this one, we need three tracking marks that remain on the same axis in the real footage and that are as close as possible to the real floor; then we click on **Set Floor**.

We do the same with the wall if necessary. We can further tweak the scene with the other options in the **Reconstruction** menu to set the X and Y axes if we need.

The last parameter we need to define is the actual distance between two real points. That's why it was important to collect as much information as we could during the shooting of the footage so we can apply this information to these options. Let's define the scale by selecting two tracking marks between which we know the distance and clicking on **Set Scale**. We can now define the size on the left-side panel under the **Set Scale** section.

Now we should have something quite close to the original footage but in our 3D scene. We could add some 3D geometry and play with it, but maybe we would need to tweak manually the origin point in the 3D viewport until it matches the perspective and the size of the objects we want. There are no formulas here—just move a little bit the origin point until what you see in the viewport makes sense to you. Usually it's quite fast to fix small issues with the perspective just by moving the origin point a little bit.

As a final note in this process, I would suggest dropping some 3D elements in some areas we are going to use to see if those objects perform well during the entire sequence. If the result is not convincing, keep tweaking the origin point in the 3D viewport until you are happy with the result. Then we can proceed with the next stage: scene setup.

Plane Track

This is a different technique that we won't use in the example for this book, but I will explain it because it can be very useful for other projects. Basically a *plane track* allows us to place or replace an element in a particular dimensional plane. For example, we could replace an advertisement banner from a shop in our footage or we could replace a cell phone screen—anything that remains in the same dimensional plane.

The good thing about using this tracker is that we are not forced to adjust our tracking marks to match the plane we want to use. As long as the tracking marks are on the same dimensional plane, we can always adjust our plane track in the position we need.

Let's see an example:

We need four tracking marks so we can apply the plane track. They don't have to be in the position we need as long as these marks stay on the same dimensional plane—in this case, the wall.

Once we have our four marks tracked, we can go to the **Plane Track** section on our **Solve** panel on the left side of the screen and click on **Create Plane Track**.

Now we should see something like this:

That's our plane track at its default position.

We can adjust the corners in the way we need manually:

Notice that now we can play back our footage and the plane should match our footage perfectly.

On the right panel we can find some interesting options as well:

By clicking on the **Auto Keyframe** button, we can manually adjust the corners of our plane track in case we have some problem. Another interesting option is the **Image** field. To use it, we need to load an image in the **Image Editor**.

If we select the image we loaded in the **Image Editor** in **Plane Track** settings, we can preview on the viewport any image we want:

This is mainly for preview purposes. We will see later on how to use this data in a final composition.

Summary

This chapter is a bit technical, and for some people it might be challenging at the beginning. But tracking is a very nice tool to know, and it's worth the effort to learn how to do it in the right way so we can expand our toolset and be more creative in our productions. It's important to keep in mind that it's hard to get a perfect track when you are just beginning to learn this technique. It requires practice and experience, so my final suggestion is to keep working on tracking shots even if they are simple tests or something basic just to gain experience and get used to these options. When I did my first tracking, I did many things wrong and the results were far from being good, but today I'm using this technique almost every day so it's no longer a problem. Keep trying hard with the tracking tools until you have mastered them; 3D tracking is a really sweet feature, too.

4

SCENE SETUP

If we already have a nice tracking solution, the next step is to set up the scene in a proper way to get the right plates to use in post-production. In this chapter we're going to see how to set up the scene and a few tricks to avoid problems. Keep in mind that this book is not about modeling or animation, so previous knowledge about this might be necessary.

World Creation

Now that we have an empty scene with the right camera, let's start adding some objects or elements we're going to use in the next steps. There are a few important steps to follow. It is important in complex projects to keep everything organized so we can more easily handle the situation if it gets complicated. The most useful tool for this is the layer manager:

We can move elements from one layer to another just by pressing the **M** key and then selecting the layer where we want to place the element. Also you can organize your bones and other animation helpers in the armature visibility manager:

We are going to use these tools in the next chapter to generate the layers we need in the composition stage.

Setting up Elements

For this book I created an example scene to go through all the stages. I modeled a robot and I created some animations for it.

Usually when the tracking camera is solved, the camera won't be aligned correctly:

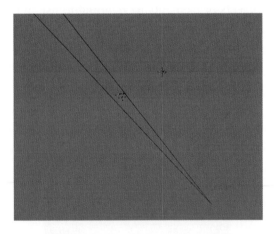

It's always better to keep all the elements on the correct axis because this makes it much easier to work with objects and is especially useful for animations. To correct this issue, we can select the origin track point in the 3D viewport and manually adjust to the desired coordinates. You can also parent the camera to an empty object and then move the entire camera setup to the location you need.

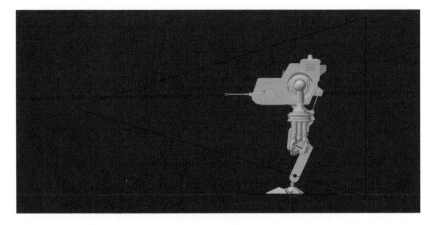

Of course, objects have to be placed on the correct axis to avoid problems:

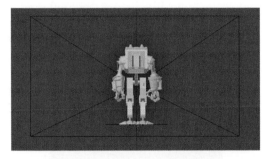

Now that we have the camera and the objects in the right positions, we can create some supporting objects for the composition, like a 3D ground to receive shadows:

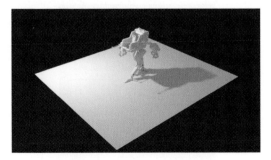

We can also create some occluding objects by creating some cutouts in the plates like a matte pass for our elements:

We are going to see how to set up these elements for rendering in the next chapter, so for this chapter we need to set up the models so that we can proceed to the next stage. Just keep in mind that you might need some of these elements to help you later on during the composition.

A useful tool is the Open GL preview, which is a very fast way to preview what our scene looks like before the final render:

Remember to set up the output settings before using the Open GL preview to generate the file in the format you need:

Lighting

How to light up your scene in the correct way is one of the most important things to learn in 3D. By setting up the lights in the right way, we
can not only increase the quality of our final images but also decrease
the render times. Keeping low render times is very important in any
production, especially if you're doing animations. This is particularly
critical if you try to achieve realistic lighting and rendering, due to the
fact that achieving a realistic look requires more complex calculations.

In the example for this book, we are trying to approach a realistic
production so we are going to use a combination of three different lighting techniques that together provide the look we are trying to achieve.

The basic setup for lighting is the manual method of placing light
sources where we think they can best help us achieve our goals.
Different types of lights provide different results:

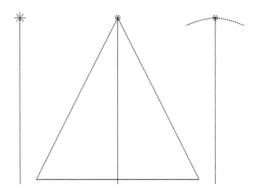

There are also *mesh lights*. We can use any object to emit light from, but keep in mind the normals of the object to direct the light in the way you want. Here is an example of a scene lighted by a mesh emit object only, with no additional lights:

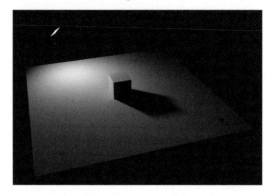

The final lighting technique we can use is IBL (image-based lighting). We can select a panoramic image to light up a scene in a very accurate way. It will also provide us with nice reflections. By using an HDR image, we will be able to calculate the lighting in a more accurate way as it contains more lighting information with different expositions on the same file:

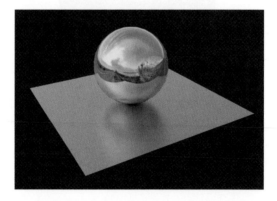

Make sure you check the **Multiple Importance** option in the **World** panel to speed up the rendering if you use IBL or HDR lighting:

▼ Settings

Surface: Volume:

☑ Multiple Importance   Equiangular

◄ Map Resolution: 256 ►   ■ Homogeneous

In the robot example, I used a combination of these techniques. The main light is an IBL setup, whereas I used a manual light to light up some areas and mesh lights for some of the lights that the robot has.

Summary

The main goal in this chapter was to understand the different types of lights and learn how to set up our scene. From here, we can jump into the next chapter, where we will be dealing with different rendering techniques to get the elements we will need for the composition.

5
RENDERING

It is time to generate the plates we are going to use in the composition. In this stage we are going to see how to set up the render properties and layers. We are also going to see the different options for rendering.

Internal Render vs. Cycles Render

Blender has two totally different render engines integrated in the main package: Blender Internal and Cycles. While Blender Internal is a very mature render engine with several years of development behind it, Cycles is a much newer render engine and the internal architecture is totally different, in some ways better but in other ways more limited in the actual status.

The following is a short list of the benefits and limitations of these two render engines:

Internal Render Pros and Cons

- More flexible generating render passes
- Light groups
- Noise-free renders
- Slow render engine in several situations
- Lack of advanced rendering algorithms
- CPU only

Cycles Render Pros and Cons

- CPU and multi-GPU acceleration base
- Advance node-based materials and OSL (Open Shading Language)
- More realistic rendering algorithms
- Render passes produce artifacts when using motion blur

Due to the fact that for the example for this book I want to explain the most common techniques and Cycles is more frequently used these days, we will continue with Cycles for this rendering job.

Rendering with Layers

Rendering with layers is a very powerful and useful feature in almost any production. With this method, instead of a single pass render, we can have more options to improve the final look of our project and gain more control over the elements we use.

If we set up our scene in the right way, we can tweak many things without having to rerender the whole scene and we can apply effects in a way that wouldn't be possible with a single pass render.

To do that, we can use the **Render Layers** panel.

There are four different ways to control how the layers are working in our scene:

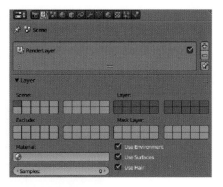

- **Scene**: All the elements in this section are being calculated in the desired layers, including reflections, lights, shadows, and so on.
- **Layer**: In this section you can separate the elements into different layers, which are calculated individually.
- **Exclude**: Elements in this section are not being calculated and are not going to provide reflections, shadows, or any other global calculation.
- **Mask Layers**: By adding objects in this section we create a cutout in the render pass, also called an alpha mask or matte. Keep in mind that not only does this create an alpha mask on top of the layer but also the elements in this section are included in the global calculations including reflection, shadows, and so on.

Let's see how this works with a simple example:

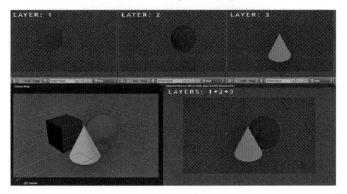

We placed three different objects in three different layers. We also created another layer that combines all three layers in one. This may look a little bit odd at the beginning, but in postproduction we would have much more control over every single element without having to rerender the scene. It's especially useful for complex scenes. Now let's look at an example of applying options to these layers:

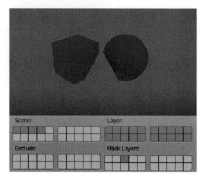

In this example we set up the cone layer, which is in layer number 3, to create a mask in the overall render pass.

Now let's see another one:

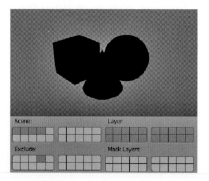

Here we have the light of the scene in layer number 4 and we selected that layer in the **Exclude** section; now the light is no longer being calculated. We can isolate elements by doing this.

As you can see, by combining different layers we have a great deal of control over what we want to render and how. Layering is a very powerful tool, and later we will look more closely at how to work with different layers.

Understanding the Render Passes

By now we know how to separate elements in different layers to have more control over the rendering, but now let's see how to gain even more control during postproduction by setting up render passes.

With render passes we can separate rendering information into different channels and tweak them individually in postproduction—for example, if we want to control how many shadows are going to be cast in the final image, relight an element, or retexture an object without having to rerender the entire scene. It's a powerful, time-saving tool that can help us improve the final quality.

As we know Blender has two built-in render engines. Let's have a look at the render passes panel for Blender Internal:

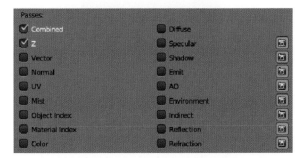

And for Cycles:

As you can see in these panels, there are many settings to be activated, but sometimes we don't need so many for a specific render. Let's see one by one how these passes work. The main difference between the Blender Internal render engine and Cycles is that Cycles splits the

Diffuse, Glossy, Transmission, and **Subsurface** passes into three different ones. We will see later on how to combine all these passes in the composition.

Combined (RGBA)

This is the most commonly used pass. It is a standard RGB (red, green, and blue) channel with an alpha channel for masking purposes (RGBA).

This is how the alpha channel looks by itself:

We will use this channel for isolated areas in postproduction to apply effects only where the white parts are visible or to create simple compositions between layers.

Depth (Z)

This channel can be applied in different ways. We can use this channel to generate a depth of field effect or even fog/mist effects.

Ambient Occlusion (AO)

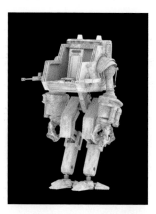

Ambient occlusion is a method that generates darkness in particular areas of our scene, usually in the corners between different objects. We can use this channel to generate some kind of dirt pass or to improve the shadows in a different way. To control this effect, we have to go to the **World** section:

In this panel we can control how much ambient occlusion we want to apply to our scene and also the distance.

Shadow

With this channel we can control how the shadows are applied in the render. We can later on tweak this channel to adjust the intensity or the color of the shadows until we have the results we want.

Vector

The vector channel is generated based on the motion of the elements in our scene. If an object has some kind of motion, then it will appear in this channel with these apparently random colors; then we can use this channel in postproduction to generate motion blur. Keep in mind that by using this technique you can very quickly produce motion blur effects in your renders, but the result is not going to be as accurate as real motion blur created during the rendering.

Normal

This is a very powerful channel. Thanks to this channel, we can relight our scene in postproduction without having to rerender; by combining this channel with the **Color** pass and others, we can have almost immediate feedback for tweaking the scene in a very flexible way from a lighting point of view. This can be a big time-saver if you have a client who wants you to tweak some lighting and you have to deliver a quick turnaround.

Object Index

With this useful channel, we can isolate objects in the compositor as if they were in individual alpha channels, so we can then tweak only the parts we need in postproduction and apply any effect individually.

To apply this method, we have to go to the **Object** panel and assign a particular index to the object we want to isolate:

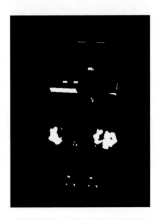

Material Index

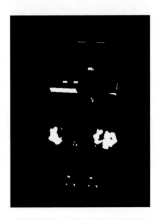

This channel is the same as the previous one but is used to isolate materials from different objects. To assign the material index, we need to go to the **Material** panel:

UV

This channel considers how textures are applied to our scene or objects, so we can retexture an object without rerendering at all.

That is basically all about channels. We will see practical examples in Chapter 7 to get more familiar with these techniques.

Formats

Now that we know how the channels and layers work, we need to understand the basics about formats and explore a few suggestions. Basically there are two types of formats: basic channel and multichannel.

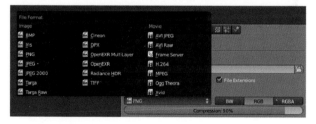

Basic Channel Format

This type of format is basically an RGB or RGBA container. Some of these formats, such as the JPEG, are compressed, which is not very good if we want to work with the best quality possible. If we want to use this kind of format without losing so much quality, we can always use PNG, TGA, or similar files, which provide a noncompressed way to store the information and also provide an alpha channel.

Multichannel Format

This format is very useful if you are looking for quality and organization. You can store as many channels as the ones described in the previous section but in a single file! You can also store the information without compression and with the highest bit rates, so this should be the way to go if you want the best quality possible and want to keep everything organized in just one file.

On the negative side, we need to consider that due to the fact that these formats store a large amount of information, the file size is usually very large as well.

My suggestions are to use PNG sequences for standard quality and EXR multichannel if you are dealing with something more professional. I also suggest that you avoid movie formats due to the limitations in some codecs and the overall lack of quality, except if you work in RAW format.

Another problem with the movie formats is that if the software crashes, your file will be corrupted; however, if you use image sequences as output, then you can always continue rendering from the frame where it crashed.

To give you an idea about file size, the example for this book is 215 frames and I'm using the EXR format with all the channels stored in the file. Every frame is 200 MB, so that's a total of approximately 43 GB for just 9 seconds of footage.

Render Settings

Let's have a quick look at the render settings. I'm not going to explain point by point all the settings because the goal of this book is not to focus on rendering. However, we will look at the most important ones.

Render Device

As we are using Cycles for our example, we may use either CPU or GPU. There are some memory limitations with GPU if we need to render very complex scenes, but on the positive side, if your graphics card is good enough, you could render the scene much faster than with your CPU. There are pros and cons with both, so choose whatever performs better with your hardware.

Render

Render	Animation	Audio

Display: Image Editor
Feature Set: Supported
Device: GPU Compute

▼ Dimensions

Render Presets

Resolution:		Frame Range:	
X:	1920 px	Start Frame:	28
Y:	1080 px	End Frame:	29
	150%	Frame Step:	2
Aspect Ratio:		Frame Rate:	
X:	1.000	24 fps	
Y:	1.000	Time Remapping:	
Border	Crop	Old: 100	New: 100

▼ Sampling

Sampling Presets

Path Tracing		Square Samples	
Settings:		Samples:	
Seed:	0	Render:	200
Clamp Direct:	5.00	Preview:	200
Clamp Indirect:	1.00		

▼ Light Paths

Integrator Presets

Transparency:		Bounces:	
Max:	8	Max:	2
Min:	8	Min:	1
Shadows		Diffuse:	4
Reflective Caustics		Glossy:	4
Refractive Caustics		Transmission:	12
Filter Glossy:	0.00	Volume:	1

▼ Film

Exposure:	1.00	Gaussian	
Transparent		Width:	2.50

Dimensions

This is quite straightforward to understand. Just set the resolution and the frame rate you need.

Sampling

The purpose of this section is to set up the number of passes we want to calculate and then the process will stop at the user's defined value. We can set the samples for the final render and for the preview.

Light Paths

Here we can set up how many calculations we want for each individual setting. By tweaking these parameters, we can reduce the render times at the cost of quality. It is recommended to spend some time doing tests with different values to see which ones work best in our scene before we do the final render.

Film

The most important setting here is **Transparent**. We need to enable this option if we want to generate an alpha channel during the render; otherwise, our scene would render as a flat pass with a background.

Also, you can adjust the exposition by the parameter **Exposure**, but it's better to adjust this directly through the lights settings or with the compositor during postproduction. Use this option if you just want a quick way to tweak the overall lighting.

Overscan

This topic can be avoided depending on your shot, but I thought it was important to include due to the fact that it is essential in many visual effects productions. If you don't know what overscan is or why you should be concerned, you should read this just in case you need overscan in your current project or in future projects.

This technique is related to the lens calibration we did in Chapter 3. Basically, we have to keep in mind that most of the render engines cannot produce images with distortion in the same way as real lenses. That's why we used the calibration sheet and the lens distortion settings in the tracking. The next step is setting up the render in a way that can produce images that are suitable for composition while we match the original lens distortion in our footage.

Let's see an example of what overscan is and how it works. This is how a standard render looks in the viewport:

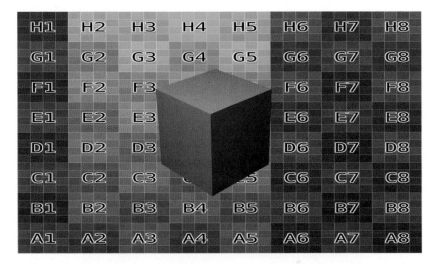

And this is how the same render looks once we apply the distortion settings from our lens calibration tool in the tracking module:

As we can see, now there is an empty space around the image; when we compose our render in the original footage, we won't be able to cover the entire frame. We need to generate our image with larger dimensions so that we can use that extra buffer to apply the correct lens distortion without having this empty space around our image.

To generate this extra buffer in our renders, we need to use a technique called *overscan*. Some render engines have this option in the settings, but in Blender there's no actual setting for this, so we need to manually configure Blender to render our scene to match the overscan technique.

The way to do this is by changing two values: the resolution scale and the sensor size on the camera.

In this example we add 10% of overscan to our render. In the **Resolution** section we just need to add the extra percentage we want to use, and in the **Camera** section we can just change the sensor size to add the same percentage. For example, if the original sensor size was 32, we multiply by 1.10 (for the extra 10% we are adding) so it will turn into 35.20.

Here it is the original frame without overscan:

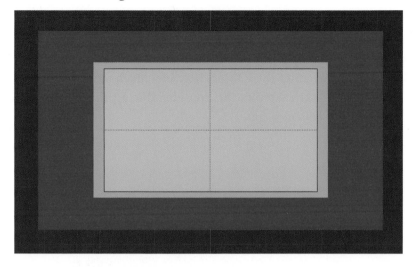

And here is the same frame with overscan:

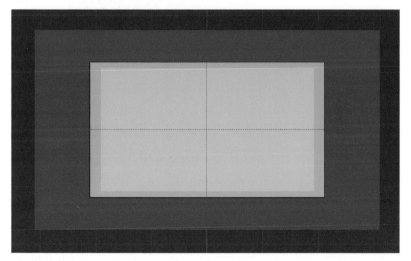

Notice how the cyan area (original render size) becomes as big as the green area (10% overscan). The grid shows the limits of the image. The red area shows what won't be rendered at all.

Summary

We covered many topics in this chapter, but they are all related to the composition work that we are going to see in Chapter 7. This chapter was designed to explain how all these passes and layers work, as we are going to encounter these topics later in a much more detailed way and with practical examples. So consider this a primer for what is coming in subsequent pages.

6
MASKING

Now that we have all the 3D plates ready, we need to work on the real footage that will be used in the composition, the same one we used during the tracking stage. Because we created some tracking marks to achieve better tracking on several locations, we need to remove these marks to have a clean plate for compositing. We cannot remove the marks directly by using a chroma key effect because other tones and elements need to be removed from the plate as well, so to clean this plate we are going to use the masking tool. We will start with a plate like this:

And we will turn it into something like this:

We use a very bright color to differentiate the subject from the background, so it is easier to see any artifact or problem with our mask; then we can change this color to any other background with total confidence in the quality of our mask.

Starting to Mask

Let's start by going to the mask editor. The interface is the same as the one we used for the tracking:

This time, however, we need to click on the pop-up menu to change to the mask editor:

And we click on **New**:

Nothing really changes in the user interface, but now Blender is set up to start working with masks. To place the first point, just press **Ctrl** and the left mouse button and you will see how one point is created. Find another area to continue drawing a silhouette over the subject you want to mask by repeating the same combination to add more points.

One suggestion is to create the points around the subject in a counterclockwise direction to ensure that the mask is pointing in the right direction to play later on with the feather options.

If you need to correct some points, you can use the standard hotkeys in Blender to select, grab, or perform any other necessary operation on the points.

To close the mask, press **Alt+C**:

We are actually creating a basic mask. We will add some refinements later on. We can even create multiple masks to define areas in a better way. For the moment, we will focus on creating a base mask.

The next step is to move through the frames and adjust the mask for the actual frame. Once we have adjusted the mask, we press **I** to insert a keyframe; if we need to delete a keyframe, we can press **Alt+I**.

We don't have to go through this process for each frame. You can do it every five or ten frames or so, but the frequency mostly depends on the footage you are working on.

By pressing **V** we can access a menu to change the handle type for each point:

Clean Plate Preview

We know how to work with masks, but now we need to see the results to do finer adjustments to get a clean plate after this process. To do this, I suggest splitting the view and having on one side the mask editor and on the other side the node editor:

This makes it much easier to adjust things with the mask editor and see the results in the node editor. We could also use the image editor later on to output the final image while we keep working with the masks.

For now let's set up a basic chroma key workspace. It doesn't have to be perfect, just usable enough to at least give us a better idea of what we are doing while we are working in the mask editor. Don't forget to turn on **Use Nodes** and **Backdrop** before the next steps.

We are not going to go over complex details about nodes and other stuff, as this chapter is mainly about masking. In the next chapter, which focuses on compositing with nodes, we will have a close look at each individual node. For now we can set up something very basic, as in the example I am going to show. If you have any trouble with keying, you might find it interesting to jump to the next chapter and read a little bit about the nodes and then continue with Chapter 6.

This is the basic setup I am using to preview the quality of my masking:

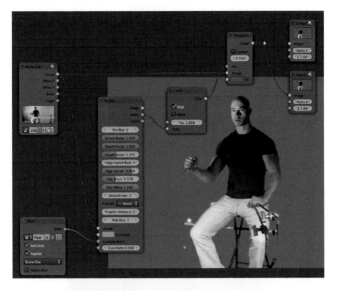

We can use the channel toolbar to preview a particular channel:

Refining the Mask

Now that we have the basic stuff and we can preview how our plate is getting clean, we can adjust a few other things. Let's talk about feathering.

We can make our mask work as a sharp shape or as a smooth shape, by selecting the masking point we want to smooth/sharpen and pressing **Alt+S**; then, when we move the mouse, we would notice how the contour of our mask is growing a secondary shape, which controls the feathering of our mask. Here is an example of a sharp mask and a smooth one:

There are additional options in the side panel to adjust a few other things about masking:

In this panel we can add additional masks into the main one and use these secondary masks to cut out or to extend the main mask. There are different options to blend the masks:

Tracking the Mask

This is a very useful technique. It basically allows us to automatically move our masks according to a tracker marker previously tracked. Let's see an example.

We want to mask this tripod in our footage, but instead of having to keyframe our mask in all the frames in our footage, we can automatically move the mask following any mark. To do this, we need to select a tracking point already tracked appropriately.

Once we have our tracking mark, we can create the mask as usual.

Finally all we have to do is select all the points in our mask and parent our mask to the tracking point:

Make sure you have previously selected the tracking point you want to use to translate the mask accordingly. If you have not, you can always go back to the tracking module to select the right one.

Now we should be able to see how our mask automatically moves with our tracking point. We can still manually tweak the mask in case we want to adjust the shape in a particular way during the footage. We can also parent mask points into tracking points, and doing this will deform the mask following the tracking marks as well. It's a very powerful tool.

So that's the basics of masking in Blender, but before we close this chapter I would like to mention an additional way to clean up a plate. You can use this alternative method as your main one or in conjunction with the masking tools to refine some areas of your footage; whichever method you use is fine if the results are good. The alternative method is called *frame-by-frame painting*.

Frame-by-Frame Painting

We can paint areas frame by frame. To do that, we need to switch to the **UV/Image Editor**.

Then we click on **Image** and **Open Image** and select the first frame or the movie file we want to use. After this, press **N** to open the side panel. If you are working with a sequence of frames instead of a movie file, you need to change the source from **Single Image** to **Image Sequence** and then select the option **Auto Refresh**. Don't forget to adjust the length of the sequence.

Now we can click on the pop-up menu to select **Paint** mode:

You will notice that a new series of options is added to the side panel:

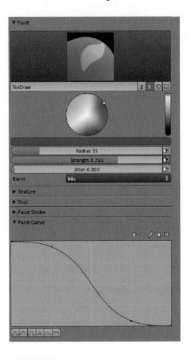

A new toolset for painting is ready for use. Now we are able to go to any frame we want and start painting all over as if we were in a 2D paint program:

Don't forget to save each frame to commit the changes. You can use the shortcut key **Alt+S** to speed up the process.

Summary

If we followed all the steps in Chapters 1 to 6, we should be in very good shape to do the final polish to our project in Chapter 7. All the plates are ready, and we have seen different techniques for having the plates in the right way for the compositing stage. In this chapter we learned two different techniques for cleaning up our footage. Now let's head into the final chapter.

COMPOSITING

It's time to get into the most important chapter of this book, the final one. This chapter is divided into two main parts: explanation of the compositing nodes and compositing the robot scene. It is divided in this way so you can have a clear idea of how to use the nodes in your own projects but also to show you a real example of how to create a composition. During this process, we will see some tips as well of how to achieve interesting effects thanks to the compositor in Blender.

First Steps

Let's jump into the compositor by selecting the **Node Editor** in the **Editor Type** button. Then we should click on the third icon at the bottom bar called **Compositing nodes** and check **Use Nodes** and **Backdrop** so we can start working with the nodes. The backdrop option allows us to see the result on the viewport once we add an **Output**

Viewer node from the **Add** menu at the bottom.

The concept around these nodes is to connect some of these nodes between an input and an output. As input we can select an image, scene, video, or other file, and then we can output the result to a spe-

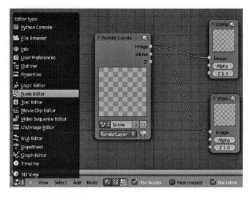

cific file/format or to the **Compositor** node. In between these connections, we can add many other nodes to tweak the image as we wish.

Nodes Overview

Blender has multiple nodes for compositing our scene. It is really important to know how each of these nodes works so we can take advantage of these utilities to create the scene in the way we want. Here is a quick overview of all the available nodes and how to use them.

Inputs

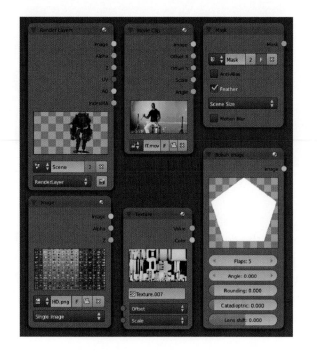

These are the first things we need in our composition. We can have multiple inputs and join them together in very different ways before we output the result.

For inputs we can use still images, image sequences, videos, masks, textures, and more.

The following sections describe the different types of inputs.

Render Layers   This input provides information from a rendered 3D scene and can include several passes.

Image   With this input we can select a file from the hard drive to be included in the composition. This file can be a single file, a sequence of images, or a movie file.

Texture   This brings a texture from the actual scene into the compositor.

Value   With the **Value** node we can create a global numeric value to share with other nodes.

RGB   Similar to the previous one, the **RGB** node generates a color value instead of a numeric value.

Time   This node is useful for animating parameters over time, even though this input was used more often in previous versions due to the lack of having keyframes in the nodes as the recent Blender versions have.

Movie Clip   This node is similar to the **Image** node, but it allows you to load a movie clip from, for example, the tracking or masking editors.

Bokeh Image   This node should be used in conjunction with **Bokeh Blur** or a similar node. It generates an image to simulate camera lens effects.

Mask   This node loads a mask layer created from the mask editor to be applied into the composition. We can use this node to affect selected areas in our composition.

Track Position   So we don't have to manually tweak the position of our elements, this node provides translation information from a tracking point to the composition; it is used in conjunction with tracking data.

Outputs

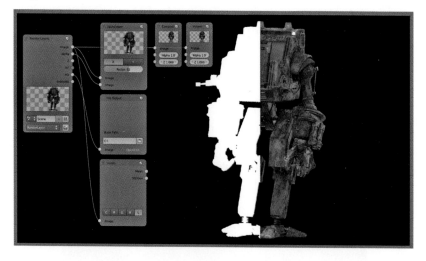

These nodes provide the final output in our composition and can be of use for previsualization purposes on the viewport.

Composite   This node brings the result from the last node connected to the final output. Usually we will use this node if there's only a single output that is predefined in the **Render Panel** in the 3D viewport.

Viewer   This is a very useful node to preview the actual stage of our composition. By attaching this node into any other one, we would see the result at that particular point. We can use the shortcut **Ctrl+Shift+left mouse button** to rapidly connect this node into the selected one.

Split Viewer   Another previsualization node, this node has two inputs so we can connect two different nodes and see on the viewport half of one and half of the other one. We can control the regions with the slider.

File Output   Similar to the **Composite** node, this node provides multiple outputs instead of having a single output of the result. By adding several of these nodes, we can customize our output formats in different ways. We can select different output settings, paths, and formats. This is very useful if we need to save several passes in different folders.

Levels   This node is used to adjust the levels in a 1D format. It has one input and two outputs: **Mean** or **Standard Deviation**, depending on how we want to apply our color correction.

Layout

These nodes are used mainly for organization purposes. We can arrange our compositor nodes in the way it makes more sense for us while keeping a clean workspace. We would need these nodes in complex compositions so we can have a clear idea of what we are doing without getting lost in all those nodes.

Frame

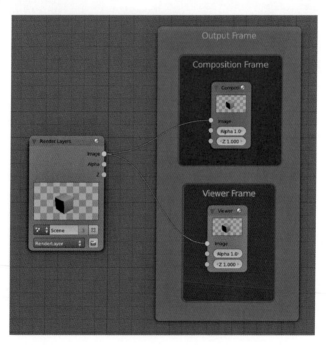

We can use a frame with our nodes so we can grab the entire frame and move all the nodes inside without having to move them individually. We can also assign colors and labels to the frame so we can arrange our composition in a better way. To remove nodes from the frame, you can press **Alt+P** to unparent the nodes from the frame and return them back to normal.

Reroute

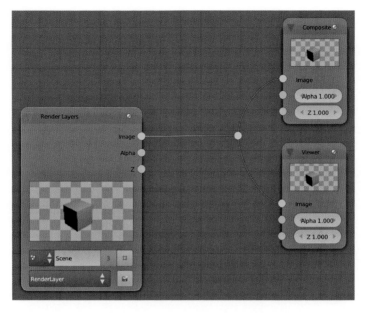

This very simple node utility is also very useful; it provides rerouting functionality so we can split or change the direction of the connections between nodes.

Switch

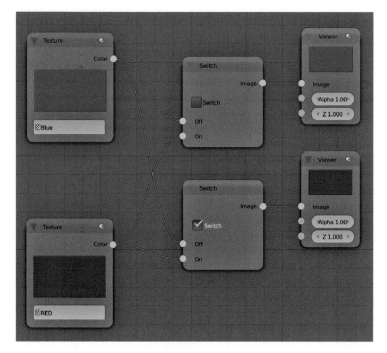

With this node we can swap connections from one node to another just by clicking in the check box.

It is useful to see different setups in a very quick way without having to plug **Viewer** nodes to specific nodes, which is good for comparisons.

Group

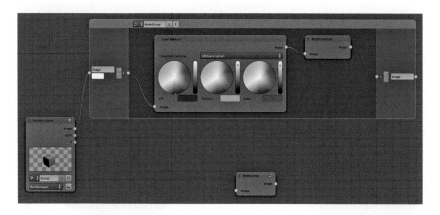

The group node is a very interesting tool to collect our nodes into a group, so that we can organize our composition much better.

Hitting the **Tab** key, we can enter or exit the selected group. If we arrange our composition with some of these groups, we can make our life much easier by just having control over a few group nodes instead of several separated nodes. We can create inputs and outputs inside the group node by just dragging a connection into one of the borders of the group, and once we are out of the group we can still have access to these connections as with a regular node.

Check the right-side panel for additional options.

Distort

With these nodes we can manipulate an image or an input in many ways. We can change basic values such as position, scale, and rotation but also create some other more complex effects.

Translate

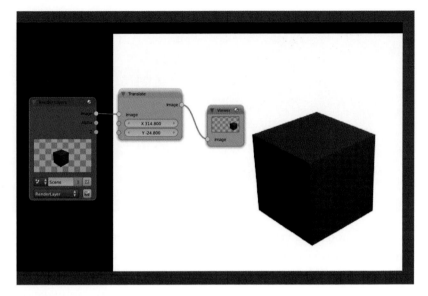

Basically we can change the position of our inputs with this node, in the X and Y coordinates.

Rotate

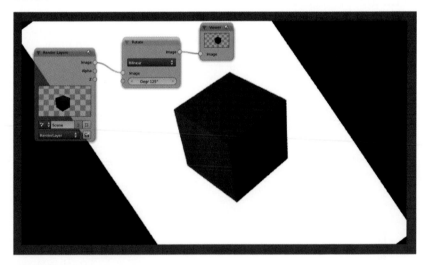

This node controls the rotation of an input. We can select three different filter modes, **Bicubic**, **Bilinear**, and **Nearest**, to choose how the pixels are calculated into the resulting output.

Scale

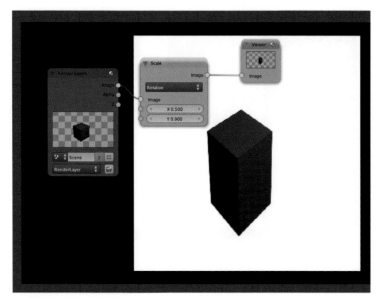

Similar to the previous ones, this node instead controls the scale of an input. We can select how to apply the scale factor in four different ways: **Render Size**, **Scene Size**, **Absolute**, and **Relative**.

Flip

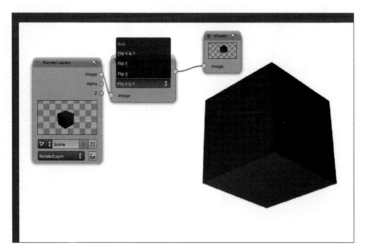

Simply use the flip node to invert the direction of an input; it can be applied in X and Y individually or in both axes at once.

Crop

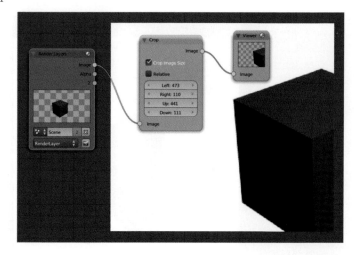

This node provides a cropping function for an input. We can define the new margins with this node by adjusting exactly how many pixels we want to crop from each side of the image.

Transform

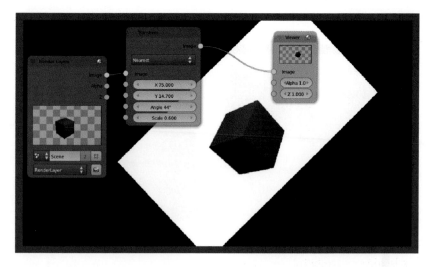

This node is a combination of the nodes **Translate**, **Rotate**, and **Scale**, but in a single node. If we need to apply more than one of these nodes to our input, we can use the **Transform** node.

Displace

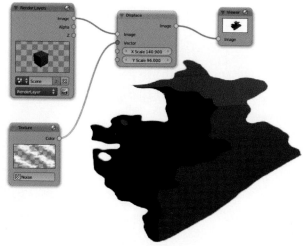

This very interesting node creates a deformation for an input based on another input, so we can control the amount of displacement we want in each axis. This could be useful, for example, to simulate heat distortion in our footage and other artistic distortion effects.

Lens Distortion

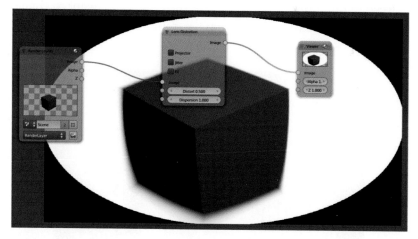

With this node, you can create a lens distortion effect. Sometimes this is nice to apply in our compositions if we want to simulate a real camera distortion effect, as all cameras have this particularity to some degree. We can control the amount and type of distortion and the dispersion to apply to our image.

Map UV

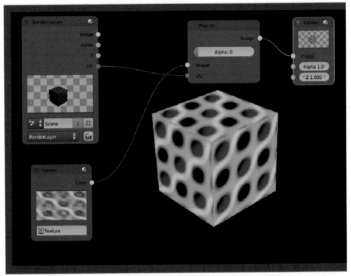

This is a very powerful node. It provides the ability to retexture an element without having to rerender the entire scene. There are two inputs: one for the texture we want to apply and a UV input to overwrite the look of our element with the new texture.

Keep in mind that we need to have the element we want to change unwrapped correctly or else we could get undesired results.

Stabilize 2D

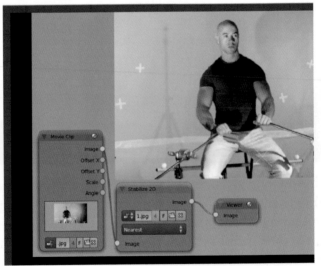

Using a tracking point from the tracking panel, this node provides stabilization to our footage. We can use just one tracking point for a 2D stabilization so we don't need to calculate a full tracking in the 3D scene if we just want to stabilize our footage.

We can also have more than one point in case we want to stabilize the rotation and the zoom factor in our footage. We can assign the points we want the **Stabilize 2D** node to use in the right-side panel of the **Movie Clip Editor**:

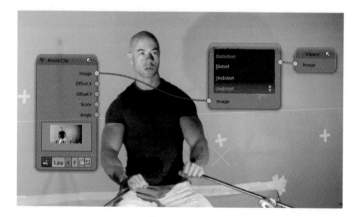

Movie Distortion

We will use this node most of the time when we want to integrate 3D elements into original footage. As we saw in the overscan description in Chapter 5, most cameras produce distortion. With this node we can apply the same distortion from our tracked footage into our 3D renders. That way, it will match the lens distortion and the composition will be more accurate.

In Chapter 5 we explained how to render with overscan to compensate for the fact that once we apply this node in our composition, it might reduce the dimensions of our 3D plates. By having that extra buffer we can apply the **Distortion** node without a problem because we should have enough pixels even if our plates get distorted and reduced.

Plane Track Deform

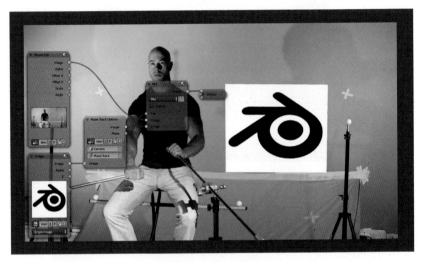

This node mainly works with a planar tracking setup. As we saw in Chapter 3 in the "Plane Track" section, we used an image to preview our planar tracking. Now, with this node, we can do a composition using that tracking data. We can assign any image to our track plane, and it will also generate an alpha channel using the **Plane** output so we can combine our track plane with any background we want.

If there is any overlap between our track plane and another element in our composition, we would add a mask on top so the track plane will look like it is behind that element.

Corner Pin

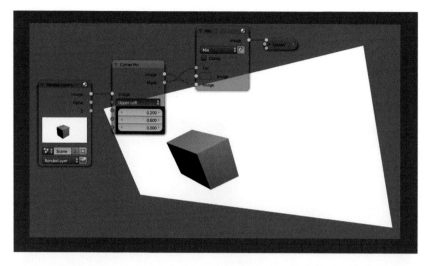

This tool is similar to the one we can find in other design programs. Basically, it allows us to distort an image by adjusting individually the corners of the image. The node has four inputs, and we can set each value by clicking on top of the drop box area. We can use the output setting **Plane** to generate a matte to combine with another image as a background.

If this node is not very intuitive for you because it uses numerical inputs, we can always plug in a **Normal** node to control the corners in a more visual way:

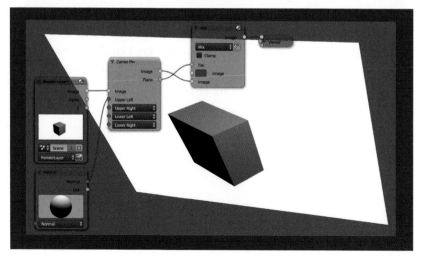

Matte

This category includes a group of nodes to control the masking and the keying of footage. There are several green screen solutions in this section.

Difference Key

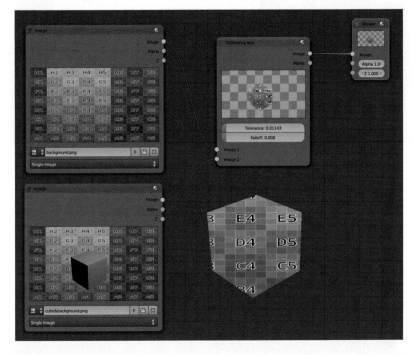

This creates a mask based on the difference of pixels from two inputs. All the pixels that are the same on both images turn transparent in the output. It also allows us to use the **Matte** output if we want to apply this mask onto a different image.

Color Spill

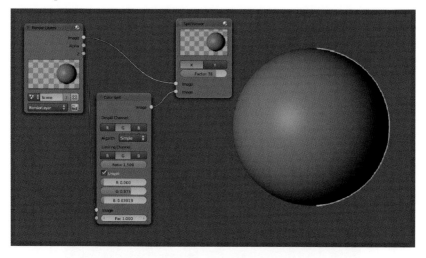

Usually when you are working on a green screen removal, you still have some spilling from the green screen background into the main element. This node decreases the amount of spill in our composition by adjusting individual color channels.

Distance Key, Chroma Key, Color Key, and Channel Key

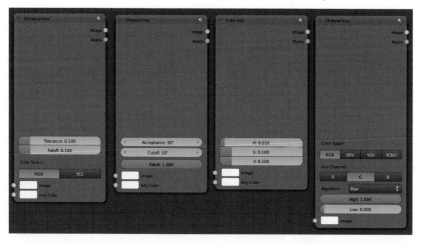

These nodes are very similar to each other. They all do chroma keying based on a key color and provide different settings to control the quality of the chroma key. However, these nodes are quite old and not as powerful as the next node we are going to see.

Keying

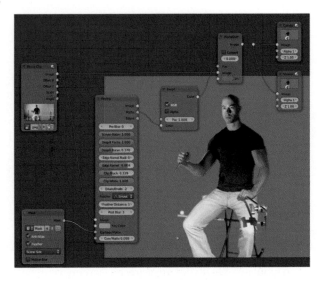

This node is a replacement for the ones we just presented. It provides more control, more quality, and more options in just one node. It also provides more control over the connected masks.

Luminance Key

With this node, we can create a mask just in the brightest areas from the input. It allows us to control the highest value and the lowest value that define the areas we want to use as a mask.

Double Edge Mask

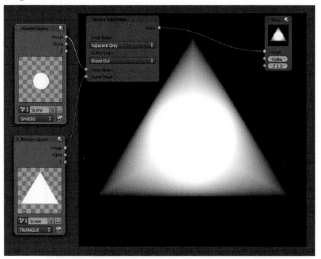

This node creates a transition between two input masks. This is very useful for advanced masking as we can create nice gradient masks to have better control over the areas we want to mask in our final composition.

Keying Screen

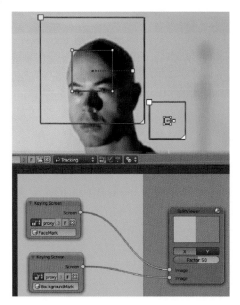

This node outputs color information based on a tracking mark. This can be useful, for example, to cover tracking marks with a similar color. As we can see in the example, we get two plain colors from two trackers.

Box Mask and Ellipse Mask

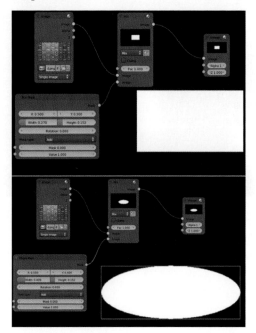

Based on the settings we want to use, this node creates a box mask or an elliptical mask. These nodes can also work in combination with other masks and provide different ways to combine them with the **Mask Type** setting.

Converter

These nodes are related to how we want to handle the channels. We can change, swap, or do other combinations with the channels as well as some other utilities to work with alpha channels.

Combine and Separate (RGBA, HSVA, YUVA, YCbCr)

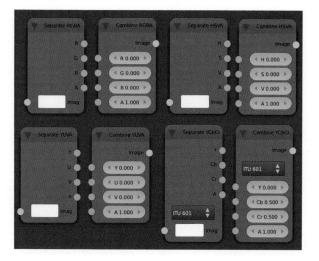

Basically, these nodes allow us to work individually with the color channels and rebuild them if we need them to work in a different way. Usually the most standard color workflow is RGBA, but if our project needs some other color workflow, we can reconnect the channels with these nodes in the way we need.

Alpha Convert

This node converts a *premultiply alpha channel* into an *alpha key* or vice versa. A premultiply alpha is a channel that is already multiplied with the RGB channels, and an alpha key channel is an independent channel with no RGB channels by multiplying the resulting alpha.

We can select how we want to work with the alpha channels in the render panel under the **Shading** section if we work with the Blender Internal render engine or in the **Film** section if we use Cycles as the render engine.

Math

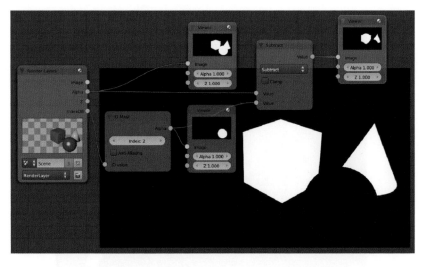

This node allows us to control the inputs in a particular way and can be used to mix or subtract inputs or control the amount of individual inputs. It is especially useful for working with alpha channels.

Here's an example of how to combine two alpha channels into one:

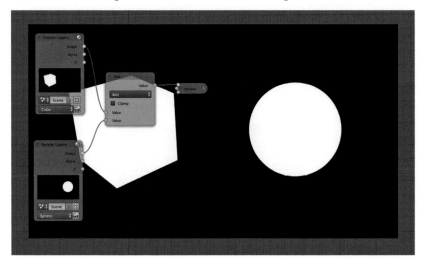

ID Mask

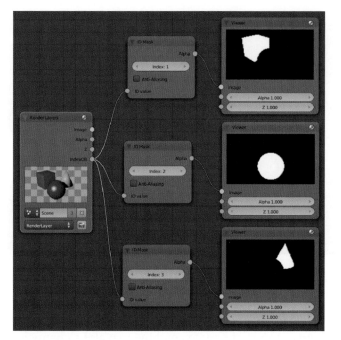

With this powerful node, we can isolate objects in our 3D scene so we can adjust them separately without affecting other parts of the scene. We can set an index for each object by the **Object Panel** in the **Relations** section (Pass Index). We can assign the same ID to more than one object if we want to adjust all the objects on the same ID at once, or we can create as many IDs as we need.

Set Alpha

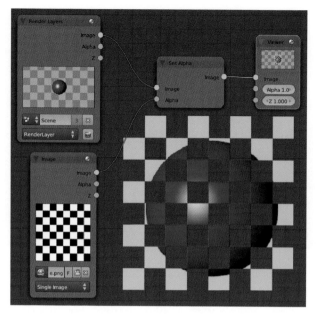

We use this simple node to set an alpha channel from another image, which is quite straightforward.

RGB to BW

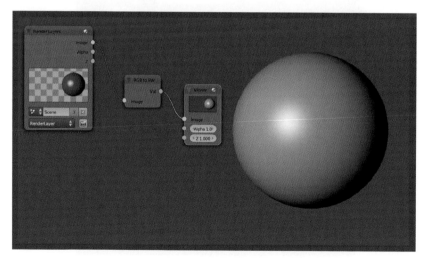

This node converts a color input (RGB) into a black-and-white (BW) output.

ColorRamp

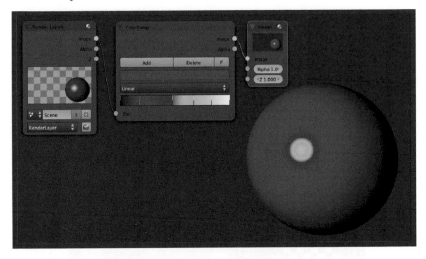

With this interesting node, we can generate a color ramp to be mixed with an input so that we can control the values of our inputs. The image above is just an example with a color channel, but this node is especially useful for controlling the depth channels with a setup like this:

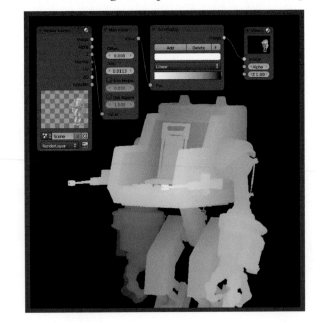

As you can see, this node is very useful for a wide range of operations.

Filter

Blender has a collection of filters to enhance our images, some blur nodes, and some others related to lens effects.

Filter

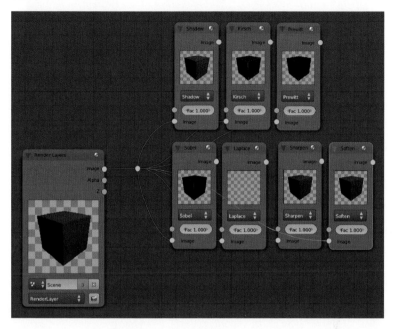

This node provides different results for our input image. It's like a group of artistic nodes, all in one single node. Maybe the most commonly used are **Sharpen** and **Soften**, but the use for these nodes depends very much on the result we want to obtain.

Blur

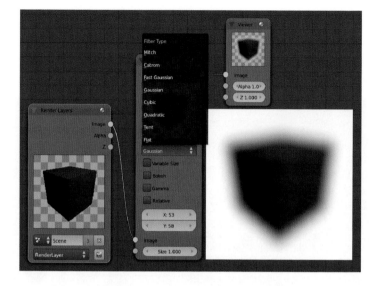

With this basic blur node, we can define how much blur we want in our input node, and we can choose between several blur methods to get the exact result we want.

Directional Blur

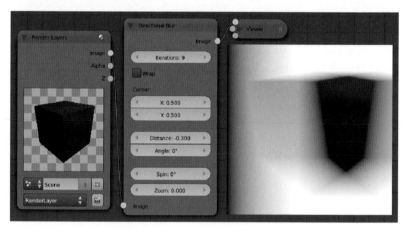

A very nice and useful blur node, this one in particular allows us to choose an angle and a distance of the blur we want. Not only that, we can also create very interesting effects by using the **Spin** and **Zoom** options.

Bilateral Blur

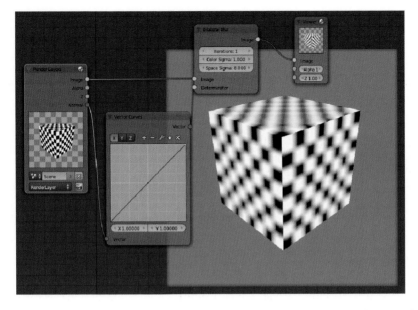

This node allows us to blur an input while preserving the edges and some detail on the borders, instead of the overall blur from other blur nodes. This node is very useful to get rid of some noise areas on our render plates by blurring them while preserving some of the detail.

You could use different render passes and combine several render passes as a determinator to keep some of the detail.

Vector Blur

This is a very quick way to generate motion blur in our creations. Once we set up our render to provide a depth channel and a vector channel, we can use these channels to blur only the parts of the scene where there is some kind of motion. This trick works very well if we want to achieve realistic images that show motion. On the other hand, if you are looking for quality you should use real motion blur by setting up the option in the **Render Panel**:

Dilate/Erode

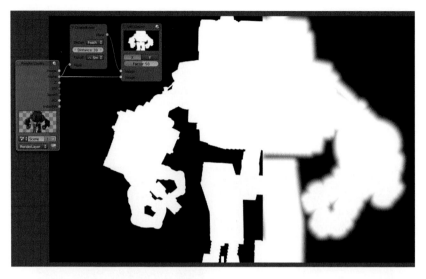

With this node we can contract or expand an input. It's especially useful to control the alpha channel in some of our elements or in some keying case where we need to adjust fine details to have perfect background removal or better integration in our scene.

Inpaint

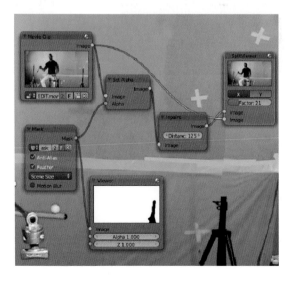

This node is useful to cover automatically some specific areas by reconstructing the selected area with the nearest pixels until it fills that area. We can use this node, for example, in a situation where we need to remove some wire work in a shot or to remove some undesired element. Don't expect to have a perfect result as it is very complicated to reconstruct areas if we don't have enough information, but for some situations it can be useful.

It is especially useful for removing tracking marks in a very quick and dirty way.

Despeckle

This is a clean-up node for some areas in our renders. If we have some artifacts or some noise in our render, we can try to use this node to clean up some of these problems. Even though it's always better to have the right plates before we start postproduction, sometimes we can still use some postproduction tools to reduce the render time or to correct some problems.

Defocus

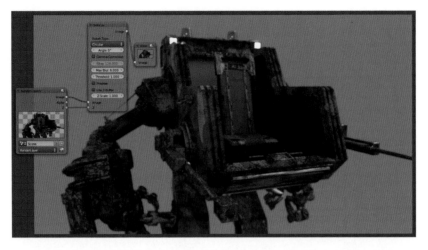

By using a depth channel in conjunction with this node, we can simulate how the real camera works with the depth of field channel. It's useful to control the depth of field during the postproduction stage, but don't forget that we can also employ this technique during the rendering as well by using Cycles; the performance is almost the same in render terms.

Also, working with depth channels directly could cause very severe artifacts and damage the quality of our final composition. Later in this chapter we will see how to address this issue and learn some workarounds.

Glare

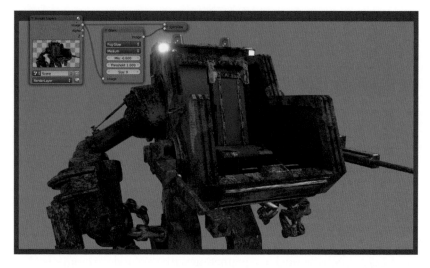

This amazing node simulates lens flares and other light effects. It has different types of effects such as **Simple Stars, Streaks, Fog Glow**, and **Ghosts**. It's based on the brightest areas of our input. Keep in mind as well that we can mix some of these lens flares together to generate a final lens flare. That way we can achieve incredible results.

Usually we would connect this node to an **ID Mask** node to isolate the areas where we want to apply our **Glare** node.

Bokeh Blur

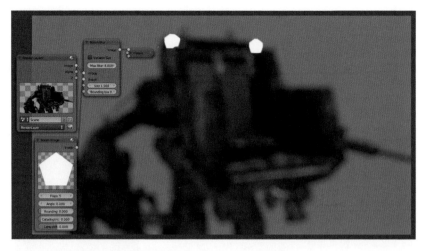

This blur node simulates the type of blur we can have with a real camera. By combining this node with a **Bokeh Image** input, we can customize how we want the blur to be processed.

Pixelate

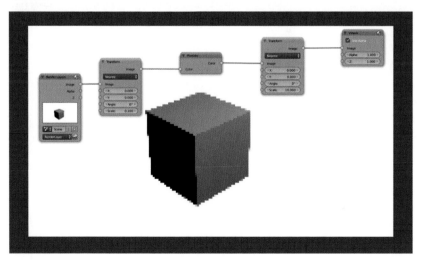

Blender usually tries to keep as much quality as possible during scaling operations. In the image above, the first **Transform** node reduces the image to 10%, and the second **Transform** node increases the image to the size it was before. As I said, Blender tries to keep as much quality as possible so we won't notice as much pixelation as we could see in 2D imaging software by doing the same procedure. So, the **Pixelate** node basically allows us to overwrite Blender's filtering to avoid pixelation, allowing us to have pixelated images in case we need this for some reason.

Sun Beams

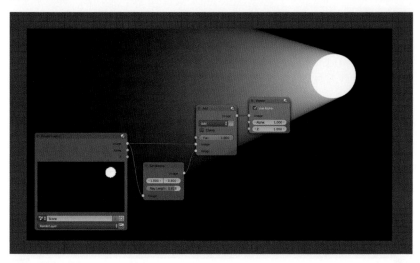

This node is really helpful to fake some volumetric lighting. It basically gets the luminance from an input and applies a fading effect in a particular direction. We can control the direction and the distance. We can also animate this if we need to by using keyframes.

Keep in mind that the generated image will have transparency so you will need to mix it with another image to have the right result.

Vector

These nodes are helpers for other ones, basically to adjust some values or to have some extra control over some particular nodes. In all the cases these nodes are very useful and very powerful. We can achieve very interesting results with them.

Normal

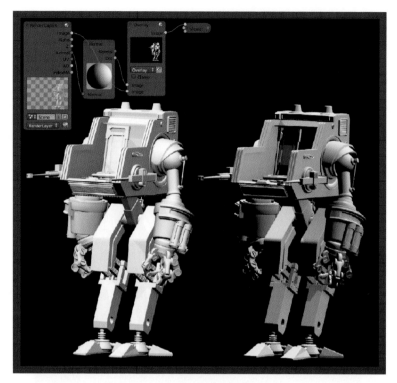

By using this node in a setup like the image above, we can adjust the shading of a particular element in our 2D composition. In other words, we can use this node, for example, to relight an element without having to rerender. If we combine this technique with some others, we can achieve immediate results without having to calculate again the entire scene, just to refine some areas of lighting. A good combination would be to use this method with the **Map UV** node.

Vector Curves

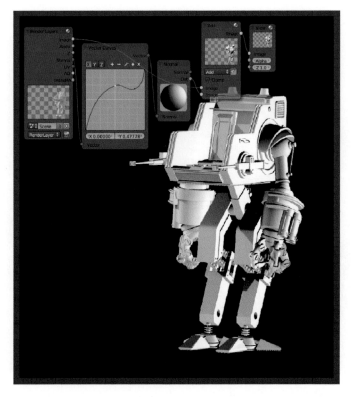

We can control the values of some channels by using this node, so we can fine tune some of the elements. This usually works in conjunction with other nodes with similar inputs and outputs.

I want to give a brief explanation about what we are going to see now with the next three nodes. They are used mainly to make adjustments in passes that need to be controlled with internal values. For example, if we plug a **Viewer** node into the Z channel to check the depth pass, we will notice that we cannot really see anything but white. That's because what we see are the depth values in an unsupported range, so we need to connect some nodes to be able to work with the range we need.

Normalize

This node provides an output of an average value based on the input. This might sound hard to understand but what it basically does is get the highest value and the lowest value and create an average value inside the supported range. It would be perfect for handling depth pass information, but this node actually creates some problems, such as flickering or artifacts, during animation, so I suggest using the nodes we are going to see next to have a better result. Use this node only for a quick preview or to have an idea of which values you might need for the **Map Value** node and for the **Map Range** node.

Map Value

This node is similar to the one we just saw except it works using numerical values. It essentially does a similar thing but provides more control over the depth channel information and also more reliable data.

Map Range

This is the node I suggest to use for one big reason: it provides the same quality as the **Map Value** node but this one uses real distance values so we can adjust these settings in a much more precise way.

To get the distance values, we can use the **Distance** value in our camera. First click on the **Limits** option and you will notice a light-yellow cross in the camera's viewport:

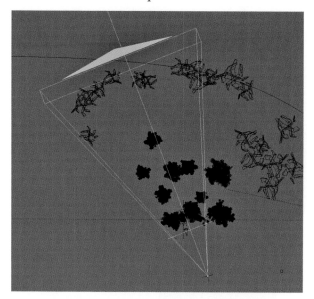

That's the position of the **Distance** value in the camera. We can use this value to set up our focal point or just to get some distance values.

All we need to do now is fill the **From Min** and **From Max** values in our **Map Range** node based on the distance that the yellow cross is telling us. You can use the **Clamp** option to crop some of the high and low values from the depth pass, and you can tweak the actual range with the **To Min** and **To Max** fields.

A final consideration about using depth passes in Blender: this software doesn't deal very well with passes at this stage. It has some severe limitations, one of which is not providing an anti-aliasing filter for the depth pass. This creates a very dirty result:

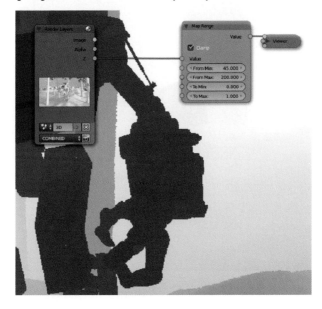

To solve this problem, we could increase our resolution two or three times just to generate this pass and on top of that we could add a **Blur** filter set as **Gaussian**:

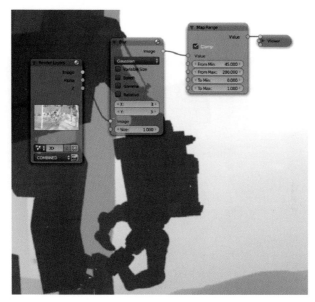

This is not the best way to do composition, but until Blender fixes this problem this could be a valid workaround. Later on we will see other methods to generate nice depth of field passes.

Color

Here we discuss the set of nodes for controlling the colors and the channels as well as some nodes for mixing inputs.

RGB Curves

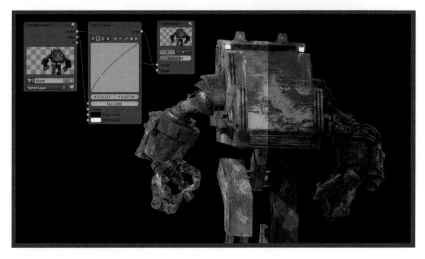

This node is quite standard in almost every 2D or 3D design application. Basically, we can control the brightest and darkest areas of a particular channel to assign a new value by modifying the RGB curve. The bottom-left corner refers to the darkest point, while the upper-right corner is the brightest. The middle part refers to mid tones.

We can adjust the overall image or just the channels we need.

Mix

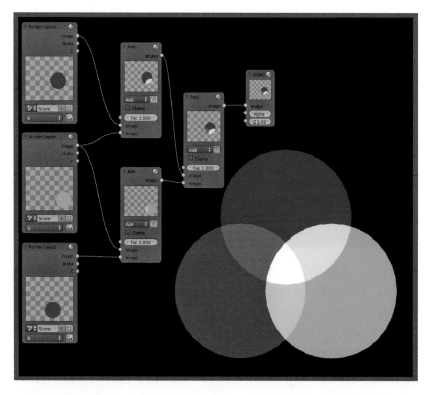

We are going to use this node most of the time, because it's very useful and very common. We have many ways to combine our inputs by using this node and all its modes. This node is necessary to recombine all the passes if we are rendering elements with separate layers. That way we can have some extra control over the entire process.

Also we will use this node to combine different elements into a single plate.

Hue Saturation Value

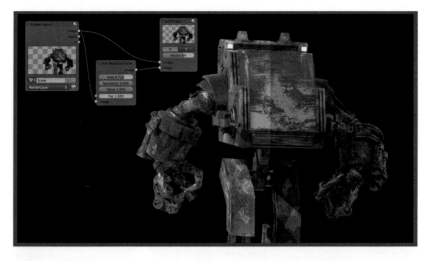

Another standard color utility, this node can be used to change the hue and saturation values, as simple as that.

Bright/Contrast

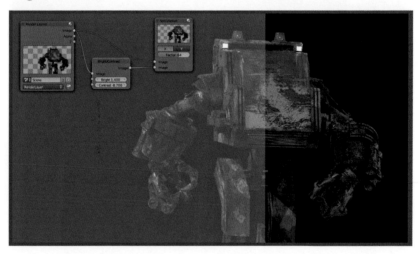

This brightness and contrast node is the same as in any 2D image retouching software.

Gamma

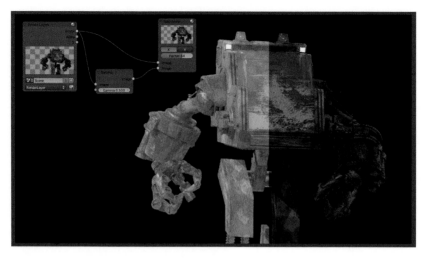

This node controls the gamma value of an input.

Invert

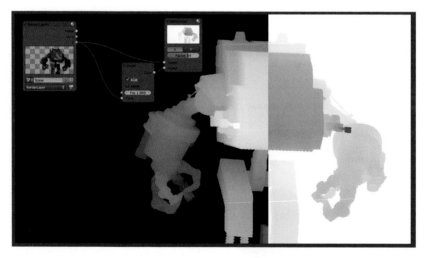

Basically, you can invert a channel (RGB or alpha) with this node. It can be useful sometimes, especially if you work with some problematic masks that need to be combined in a specific way.

AlphaOver

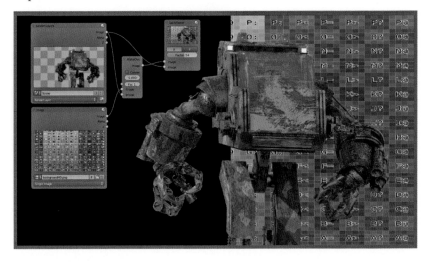

With this node we can mix two inputs based on an alpha channel, so we can create a basic composition with this node. This node also provides the option to apply the alpha as a key or as a premultiply.

Z Combine

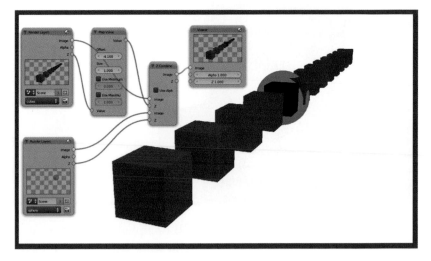

This powerful node creates compositions based on a depth channel. We can create fog or similar atmospheric effects with this node or use it for compositing elements, as in the image above.

Keep in mind the problem with the depth channels I mentioned before. Some workaround explained in this book might be necessary to get a better final image.

Color Balance

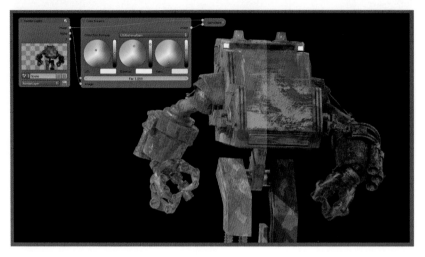

With this node for color correction, we can control the **Lift**, the **Gamma**, and the **Gain**. By combining this node with some other color nodes, we can have a lot of control over the look of an element.

Hue Correct

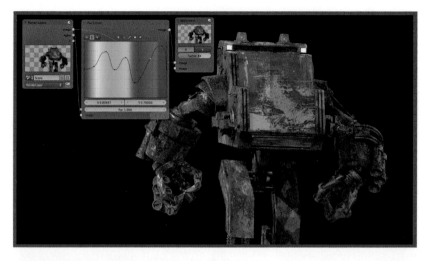

Another color tool for color correction, with this node we can control not only the **Hue** but the **Saturation** and the **Value** (brightness) as well.

Tonemap

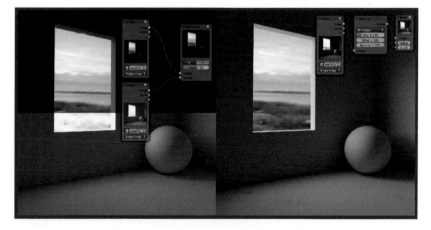

This node is basically for adjusting a high dynamic range image (HDR or HDRI). As these formats contain additional information for the lighting, they need to use specific tools to adjust the values. So, with this node we can adjust these values for this image format.

Color Correction

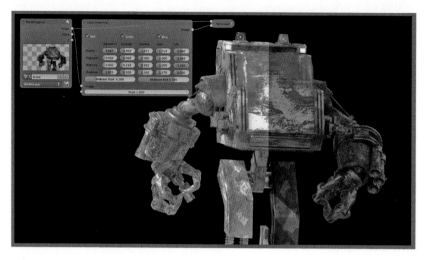

This node is similar to the previous color correction nodes, but in this case it is based on numerical values.

Compositing the Scene

Now that we know how to use all the nodes and what result we get from each individual node, let's see an example of using a combination of nodes to finish the project. We have been following the project of the robot from previous stages, and it's time to commit all the previous steps into the final result. We can start to set up the basic elements for the scene. In this case we're going to use four inputs: the 3D robot element, the actor footage, the glass, and the background. This is a very basic setup to see how all these elements works together:

Even though this is not the final version of our node tree, the idea of this setup is just to block the basic stuff we are going to use later on. First we need to make sure we have everything in place, so we can then tweak individual elements.

We saw before how to prepare the scene to render with different layers. Now it's time to see how these render layers are plugged together.

Basically, we need to use the layer channels from our input node in a particular way. When we combine the layers in the right way, we can recreate the original render but with the benefit of being able to adjust individual passes without having to render again the frames. This provides a very powerful tool for tweaking the look of our scene or elements in a very detailed way.

This is a diagram of how we should plug the nodes together to recreate the original render:

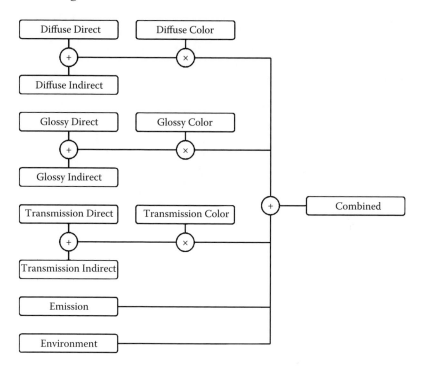

Where we see the + symbol, we would use a **Mix** node (from the color section) with a value of **Add**, which by default is set to **Mix**. Where we see the × symbol, we would use the same node but instead of **Add** we would use **Multiply**.

The previous diagram might be a little bit intimidating at first, but let's see the same diagram in our example:

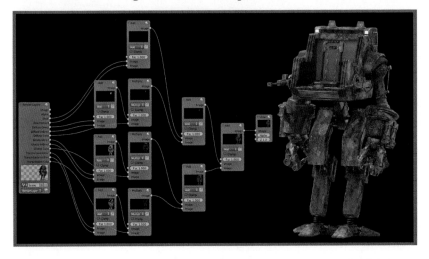

We have in this image the same connections as in the previous diagram. If we did the connections in the right way, we should have the exact image as the original render by using these nodes.

Now we can tweak individual elements with total control over each channel.

At this stage it is very important to be organized or else we might end up having a lot of trouble understanding our complex node tree.

In the previous image we saw that to have a basic setup for one of our elements (the robot) we used ten nodes already, so the total number of nodes could be a problem if we keep adding elements. Let's use node groups to manage our elements in a much more effective way.

We can select the nodes we want and create a group from individual nodes by pressing **Ctrl+G**:

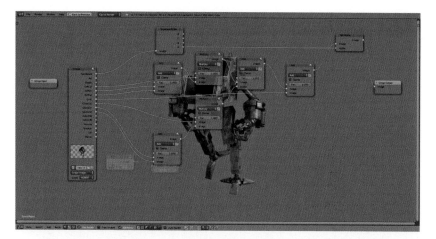

As soon as we create our group, we will notice how the background color changes. That shows us that we are inside of our group, and we cannot access other nodes until we exit from this group. To enter and exit a group, all we need to do is hit the **Tab** key.

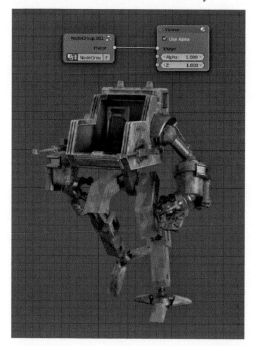

Much better now, right? We still have the availability to tweak our nodes when we want, but now we need to deal with just one node for this element.

We can label groups by colors or with custom names using the side panel:

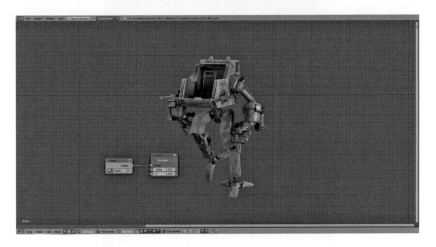

Using colors really helps to organize complex projects.

We should do the previous steps to arrange the elements we need in our composition, and we can use colors for better organization.

Without grouping our nodes, the same composition for this image would look like this:

That's why we need to start using groups and labels as soon as we can or else we will end up with a big mess. The image above shows the basic nodes needed to put the elements together. This would be the minimum to start working on.

Now that we have all the basic elements together, we could keep adding more and more nodes to have more details until we are happy with the result.

We can add some of these extra details. Let's start with an example for the lens flares.

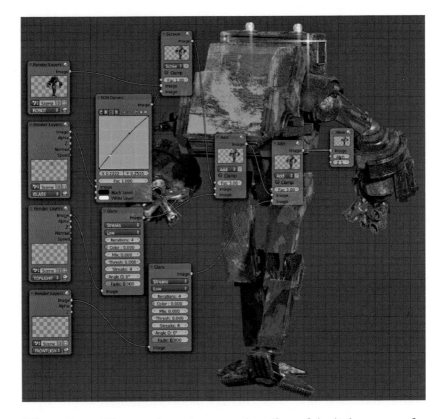

We used two **Glare** nodes to increase the effect of the light sources for the robot and then mixed them together with the **Mix** node. We can use the **Object ID** and the **Material ID** nodes to read the appropriated channels to tell the **Glare** node where to apply the effects.

Film Grain

Let's explore now two different techniques to simulate film grain. This is very important especially if we try to integrate some CG element into some real footage. Usually cameras produce some grain in the image, some cameras more than others. CG images don't produce any grain. (Don't confuse the lack of samples during rendering with grain. That type of grain shouldn't be on our final renders. We should use only clean renders and add the grain later on as we are going to see now.)

If we don't add grain to our CG elements when we add them in our composition, it will look like something not well integrated into the original footage.

Why are we showing two techniques to produce grain? Well, they are very different: one is a fake grain that works quite nicely and is easy to generate, and the other one generates the grain based on our original footage and so is usually more accurate. Sometimes you cannot use the second technique, so that's why it is good to know how to add fake grain just in case.

Fake Grain

To use this technique, we need to generate some textures to simulate the grain. Let's click on the texture node icon (1), then on the brush icon (2), click on **New** (3), and finally click on **Use Nodes**.

We should see something like this:

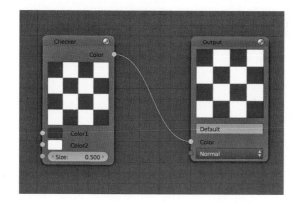

This is the default **Checker** texture. We can delete this texture so we can add the ones we need.

We need to add a noise texture:

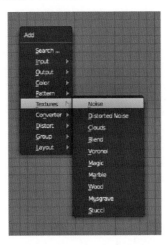

Then we duplicate this two times more, and we do the connections in this way:

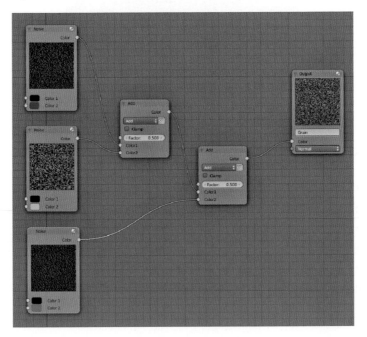

We connect the first two textures with a color mix RGB node set as **Add** with a **Factor** of 0.500. We then mix from this (combined)

node with the third one. Finally we connect the mix RGB node to the output.

Now let's add our texture to our composition:

We use a texture node and select the texture we just created. Then we plug our texture node in a filter node, and we select **Soften** with a very low **Factor**: 0.05.

After this we plug the **Soften** node into a **Mix** node from the color library. We set this node as **Color**, and for the other input to the CG layer, we want to add the grain. We can then adjust the amount of grain with the factor field in our **Mix** node. Usually a factor of 0.100 should be fine, but in the image above we raised the factor much more to show the difference clearly.

By the way, don't forget to click on the fake user icon (**F**) on the texture node to make sure the textures we created is saved in our project:

Real Grain

It's time to see how the other method to generate grain works. As I mentioned before, this second method is based on the grain from the original footage. To obtain the grain from footage we have to separate the footage and the grain.

We would need a few seconds of footage where everything remains static, including the lighting. This works best if we can film some seconds of footage with everything static before any action begins in our shot. If we don't have the chance to do this, we can also use the same camera (under the same conditions used during the shooting) to record some footage so we can capture the grain footprint of that camera. Keep in mind that if you change the settings on the camera, the grain will be different and you might generate a grain plate that has nothing to do with the plate used for the composition. So, it's recommended to film these few seconds on the same set to make sure you use the same settings and the same lighting conditions.

I recorded just a few seconds with my camera in a very extreme way to show you clearly how this works:

This is completely static footage, but when we play footage like this we can see how the grain is different from one frame to another. Now we are going to separate the grain from the footage so we can use that grain to composite our CG elements.

Let's create some nodes in this way:

As you can see in the image, we have two inputs that are the same footage but with a little offset in the frames. By using the offset, we make sure we generate grain in each frame that doesn't interfere directly with the same grain in that frame, as we are going to separate the static pixels.

We also checked the **Cyclic** option so we can reuse this grain for any length we would need for our footage. The next step is to combine both inputs with a **Math** node from the Converter library. We set up this node as a **Logarithm**, and then we connect this to a **ColorRamp** node. In my case I flipped this node and I darkened a little bit the white and offset the black, but every footage is different so you might need to tweak this **ColorRamp** node a little bit to fit your needs.

If we check how the connections look by connecting a **Viewer** node into the **ColorRamp**, we would see something like this now:

Notice how we don't see the image anymore and all that is left now is the grain. Also notice how every frame is different. All we need to do now is just mix this grain with our CG elements using a **Mix** node set as **Screen** and we can control the amount of grain with the factor:

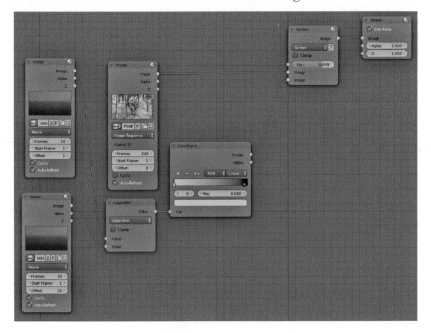

Vignetting

We can also add a vignetting effect to simulate some real lens behavior. Add this effect in a very subtle way because it is not recommended to go too extreme with this because it might produce an unpleasant look.

To add some vignetting, we can use an **Ellipse Mask** node in combination with a **Mix** node set as **Multiply** and plug in the image to which we want the vignetting to be applied.

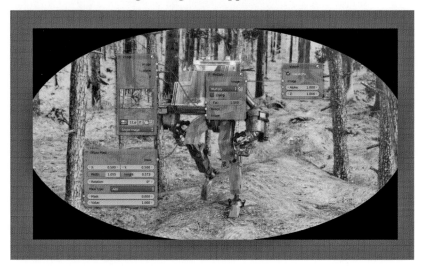

By doing this we can frame our image simulating a lens point of view, but the borders would be way too sharp.

To get rid of the sharp borders, all we need to do is add a **Blur** node and set it as **Fast Gaussian**.

With the X and Y values we can adjust the amount of blur. Also make sure that the **Blur** node is set up as **Relative** and the render size is set up correctly to avoid having undesired results. Finally we can control the overall intensity of our vignetting with the **Factor** field in the **Mix** node.

Preview

Most Blender users claim that there's no preview method to check the composition, but that's not really true. There's a way to preview footage in a similar way as other postproduction packages. It's similar to a RAM preview and it works well, but it's quite slow calculating the frames in comparison with other software. I think it can be useful sometimes if you just need to check something quickly. I still suggest that the best way will be to actually export your composition to a video file and then preview it there, even if it's in a smaller resolution.

In case you still want to know how to preview your composition using a RAM preview, here are the steps to follow.

To make this work, we will use the **Video Sequence Editor** from Blender. This module is used mostly to edit footage but we can also use it to preview our composition. Let's jump into the **Video Sequence Editor**.

Then we have to click on this icon to enable the preview on the timeline:

Now we can see the preview on top.

We need to add our scene into the timeline:

The 3D viewport now appears, but it does not show us what we want to preview.

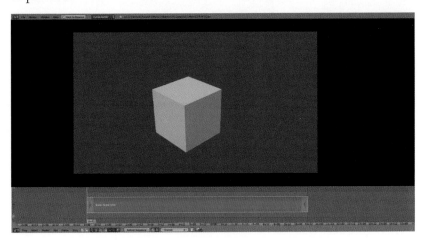

We need to override the 3D viewport and make it display the composition. To do this, we need to use the right-side panel by pressing the **N** key. In there we need to click on **Open GL Preview** to disable this option so we can then preview our composition.

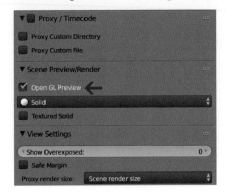

Now we can see the composition in the preview window on the **Video Sequence Editor**.

We can play the video as any other video. Notice that the first time we play the video it is going to be very slow, because Blender has to calculate all our nodes in the composition for each frame. Once one frame is calculated, it gets stored in the memory RAM, so the next time we hit **Play** it should play in real time.

This technique is very memory intensive. That's why I suggest exporting to a video file so you can avoid issues such as not having enough memory RAM to load all the frames. Still, it is a good way to preview something quickly if the composition is not terribly huge.

Rendering Limitations

Depth Pass

Cycles is a great render engine, but it has some limitations that could affect drastically our production. The main problem we can face while using Cycles is the lack of anti-aliasing filters when using depth of field and motion blur. These two features of Cycles will provide an incorrect result in the depth pass as well as in the **Material Index** pass and the **Object Index** pass.

The result for these passes will be a noisy image:

This image is perfect to show the problem, because this scene has motion blur and depth of field, the two factors that will cause our passes to not be calculated in the right way. Notice how grainy the image above is. That is not a problem of not having enough samples during the rendering. No matter how many samples you add to your render, it will produce these artifacts

Let's see first how to address the depth pass. Until Blender fixes these issues, here's a workaround.

We are going to create our own depth pass. The first step is to create a custom material in Cycles. The connections should look like this:

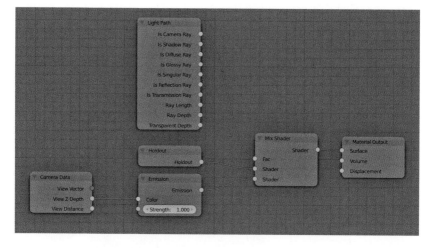

Basically, this material gets the information from the camera's depth and applies a light value base on that depth information from the camera. To avoid overlapping depth information, we use a holdout to cancel this, and we use a **Camera Ray** value as the factor for this cancellation. All this might sound a little bit confusing, but as long as you have the connection like this, it should be fine for generating our custom depth pass.

Next we have to assign this material to all the objects in our scene. The fastest way to do this is by using the global material in the **Scene** setting to overwrite all the materials with our custom one:

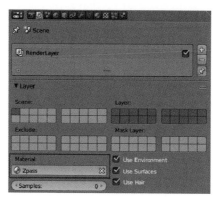

If we render our scene now, we should see mostly a white image. That white image has, in fact, depth information with an anti-aliasing filter, exactly what we need. All we need to do now is add some nodes in the compositor to prepare the depth pass for our needs.

This is the node setup we need to create:

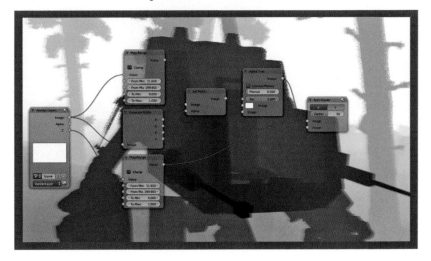

Basically, we use our image and we plug in a vector node, in this case the **Map Range** node. Now we can control the depth information to match the original depth pass. I suggest using a **Normalize** node connected to the real depth pass to compare and find out the values you will need to add in the **From Min** and **From Max** fields.

Due to the fact that we are building the depth pass from a color pass initially, we would need to recreate the background as well. To do that, we can bypass the original alpha channel and recombine this with the image after the vector node. That way we would have an exact copy of the depth pass but without the artifacts.

In the image above I used a split node so you can compare how the original depth pass (on top) looks compared to our custom depth pass (on the bottom).

Notice how grainy the upper half of the image is in comparison with the bottom one.

ID Passes

Object Index and **Material Index** are the other nodes affected when using depth of field or motion blur in cycles.

We would need a similar approach to the one we used for creating our custom depth pass, but this one is slightly easier.

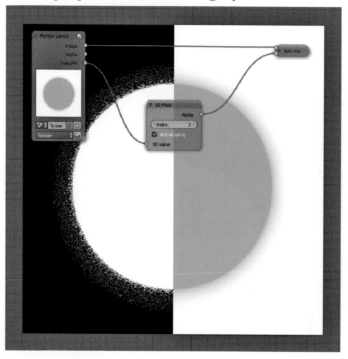

This test scene has depth of field on the camera. As we can see, it is affecting the **ID Mask,** creating a very grainy image, and it is not usable for composition. Notice the smooth borders on the original image on the right side.

Basically, we are going to generate our own **ID Mask**. All we need is a black-and-white image with the elements we want to mask out. The first step is to set our background completely to black:

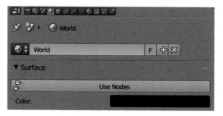

Once we have the background, we need to create a pure white material and assign it to the objects we want to use for our mask:

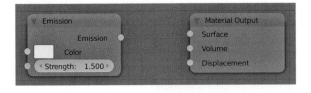

Once we have these things set up, all that is left to do is render our pass:

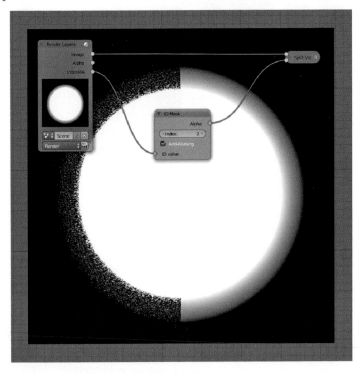

Notice now how smooth the borders on the right side are in comparison with the original ID pass.

With the depth of field workaround and with this ID pass, we should be in good shape to create our compositions in the right way.

Final Notes

At this point we should have all the elements we need together and we should be able to wrap up our project by generating the master file.

What I usually do to generate the master is output the composition as an image sequence in a format that doesn't compress the image, and then I generate an **AVI Raw** from this image sequence. I like to do it in this way because if the render crashes while generating the image sequence we can always resume the job on the same frame it crashed on. If we use a movie format and it crashes, then we won't be able to resume the job and we will need to calculate the frames from the beginning again.

I choose **AVI Raw** because it is more convenient for me to have the master in a single file while keeping the best quality possible. We should try to work in RAW formats every time we have the chance. Any other format that compresses the information will drop the quality of our work in each step of the process if we use different applications.

Summary

In this last chapter we covered all the nodes individually and we saw a practical example of how to apply some of these nodes. Of course, it would be complicated to apply the exact same workflow I showed in this book to each individual project you might face in the future, but my goal was to show the most important points during the process of creating a visual effects shot in Blender.

The best way to get used to all these nodes and workflows is by practicing constantly. That would be my last suggestion for this book.

I hope that now that we have covered all the different stages of a project, you have a better idea of how to apply all these techniques in your own projects.

Finally I just want to thank you for supporting this book and its author.

Index

141